A Twisting Journey Continues

Northern Oregon Backroads Guide to the PCT

Ed W. McBee
Two Hats Publishing, LLC
Jacksonville, Oregon

This enhanced road sign promises adventure right around the corner. Opposite: Hikers atop Tam McArthur Rim.

© 2020 Ed W. McBee
All rights reserved
All photos, maps and text by the author except where noted.

ISBN: 978-0-9904340-3-0 New edition, greatly revised.

Two Hats Publishing, LLC, Jacksonville, Oregon

Order Ed McBee's books online: Oregonbackroads.com

Book Interior & Typography: Linda Pinkham

Editors: Linda F. Kestner, Linda Pinkham

Cover Design: David Gordon

No part of this publication, except for brief quotes in printed reviews, may be reproduced, stored in a retrieval system, or transmitted in any form or by any means, electronic, mechanical, photocopying, recording, or otherwise without prior written permission from the author.

The author and publishers are not responsible for injuries or accidents sustained by readers who follow activities described in this book.
All maps and descriptions contained within this guide are subject to change and should be used alongside maps issued by the Forest Service referenced in the Guide.

This is a newly revised & updated edition of a book originally published in 2015 as "Oregon Backroads Guide to the Pacific Crest Trail, Volume 2"

May your trails be crooked, winding, lonesome, dangerous, leading to the most amazing view. May your mountains rise into and above the clouds.

—**Edward Abbey**

ACKNOWLEDGMENTS

Writing and researching *A Twisting Journey* has given me a chance to get to know many people I wouldn't ordinarily meet in my workaday world. That's certainly true of the many people I've met on the Pacific Crest Trail over the last several years. People from all points of the globe are attracted to the challenges of the 2,650 mile long trail.

The PCT is a simple concept. A linear footpath extending from Mexico to Canada is pretty straightforward, right? But no single hiker is likely to succeed without the help from other people they will meet along the way, providential help called "Trail Magic" by hikers on the PCT. There have been many people in my world who have provided their own "Magic" in the production of these books, "Book Angels" if you like.

Thanks to all of my friends in Jacksonville, Oregon who buy books and support local authors and artist. I would like to especially thank Graham Farran at Expert Properties for supporting my previous works and promoting Southern Oregon. Many more thanks to Anne Brooke and the Jacksonville Art Presence Center for promoting local authors and providing shelf space at the center, Karen Chapman at Bloomsbury Books for supporting local authors, and my friend Linda Kestner for her keen eye and constructive comments. Special, special thanks to Linda Pinkham at Linda Pinkham Publishing Services (a Commander in the Word Police) for her editing, design, and layouts.

And huge thank you and socially distanced hug to the publishing team at Lucky Valley Press, David and Ginna Gordon for their attention to detail, editing, layout, design, and guidance during the many crises of this strange year, 2020.

Thanks Book Angels!

— *Ed W. McBee*
October 2020

CONTENTS

ACKNOWLEDGMENTS	iv
MAP LIST	vi
INTRODUCTION: The Twisting Journey Continues	1
Willamette Pass to the Bridge of the Gods	2
The Lay of the Land	5
The Scenic Route	8
How to Use This Guide	10
REGION FIVE: Willamette Pass to Elk Lake	17
Route Description	19
Road Notes	25
REGION SIX: Elk Lake to Santiam Pass	55
Route Description	57
Road Notes	65
REGION SEVEN: Santiam Pass to Olallie Lake	89
Route Description	91
Road Notes	99
REGION EIGHT: Olallie Lake to Government Camp	117
Route Description	119
Road Notes	122
REGION NINE: Government Camp to the Bridge of the Gods	149
Route Description	151
Road Notes	156
FOREST ROADS INDEX	176
PLACES, PLANTS & NAME INDEX	177
AFTERWORD	186

MAPS

INTRODUCTION: The Twisting Journey Continues
Map of Western Oregon & PCT Route 4

REGION FIVE: Willamette Pass to Elk Lake
Multi-Region Map 1: Regions 5, 6, & 7......................... 16
Map R5.1: Willamette Pass to Elk Lake 24
Map R5.2: Waldo Lake & Optional 4290 Road 31
Map R5.3: Charleton Lake to Little Cultus Lake 37
Map R5.4: Crane Prairie Reservoir 47
Map R5.5: Cascade Lakes Highway 51

REGION SIX: Elk Lake to Santiam Pass
Map R6.1: Main Route 54
Map R6.2: Elk Lake to Todd Lake Trailhead 65
Map R6.3: Todd Lake to Three Creek Lake 72
Map R6.4: Sisters to Santiam Pass 79

REGION SEVEN: Santiam Pass to Olallie Lake
Map R7.1: Main Route 89
Map R7.2: Santiam Junction & Sahalie Falls 98
Map R7.3: Eastern Portion of Detroit Lake 105
Map R3.4: Breitenbush Lake & Beyond to Olallie Lake 111

REGION EIGHT: Olallie Lake to Government Camp
Multi-Region Map 2: Regions 8 & 9 116
Map R8.1: Olallie Lake to the 110 Road 126
Map R8.2: The 110 Road to Summit Lake 128
Map R8.3: Timothy Lake Area 137
Map R8.4: Little Crater & Frog Lakes Area 141
Map R4.5: Timpanogas Lake to Willamette Pass........... 163

REGION NINE: Government Camp to Bridge of the Gods
Map R9.1: Main Route 148
Map R9.2: Camp Creek to Lolo Pass 158
Map R9.3: Lolo Pass to Tucker Park 164
Map R9.4: Cascade Locks – The Bridge of the Gods......171

A TWISTING JOURNEY CONTINUES
Northern Oregon Backroads
Guide to the PCT

Mount Bachelor, west of Bend, hosts one of the most popular ski resorts in Oregon.

"What lies behind us and what lies ahead of us are tiny matters
compared to what lives within us."

— *Henry David Thoreau*

WILLAMETTE PASS TO BRIDGE OF THE GODS

Beginning at Willamette Pass, *A Twisting Journey Continues* through Oregon's high country where the companion book to this one, *A Twisting Journey, Southern Oregon Guide to the PCT* ended.

In the first book of this series, starting from the south, we traversed Oregon's Siskiyou Mountains as we followed the **Pacific Crest Trail** (PCT) from the point it enters Oregon from California, hooking up with the Cascade Mountains near Ashland, Oregon then shadowing the PCT north to Willamette Pass.

Both books are divided into "Regions" with **each region taking about a day to drive.** The first book is divided into four regions designated Regions One, Two, Three, and Four. *A Twisting Journey Continues* covers Northern Oregon in five regions starting with Region Five (Willamette Pass) and ending with Region Nine at the Bridge of the Gods. To order either book in this series go to **OregonBackroads.com** or your independent book dealer.

I was born in Kansas… maybe that's why I love the mountains so much. Don't get me wrong, I don't mean to speak ill of my birth state, but there's nothing in Kansas that compares with the stunning landscapes of the Pacific Northwest.

My family traveled extensively in the United States as I was growing up in Kansas and I eventually traveled to all 50 states. I have fond memories of fighting with my big sister in the backseat of the family station wagon as we traveled across North America. Dad was a map guy and always wanted to take the "scenic route" along the backroads. Mom was OK with that idea as long as we didn't encounter any mountains…and when we did, Mom would often threaten to get out of the car and walk the rest of the way. Fortunately, Dad never gave in to the temptation to leave her in the Rockies and we all moved from Kansas to the Seattle, Washington area in 1968.

My love for Southern Oregon began at a young age. While my family still lived in Kansas we traveled to the Seattle World's Fair (in the station wagon with the squabbling siblings) then drove south along the Pacific Highway (Old Highway 99) through Southern Oregon and California. Even at that tender age (10) I was impressed by the gorgeous mountains and hills of southern Oregon and I remember being bowled over by the sight of the glacier covered behemoth Mount Shasta in northern California, we certainly had nothing like that in Kansas.

Introduction: The Twisting Journey Continues

The ancient rocks of southern Oregon's high Siskiyous are strewn with wildflowers in early summer.

As I turned 17 (living with my parents in Mukilteo, Washington), I had the chance to return to Southern Oregon and spend time at a friend's cabin, located in the Illinois Valley near Cave Junction, Oregon. Being somewhat of a "third wheel" as my buddy pursued his girlfriend, I was given the use of a Honda Trail 90 motorcycle with a broken chain.

After fixing the chain and for about a dollar's worth of gas a day, I roamed the hills and mountains of the Siskiyou and Klamath Mountains. In awe of the beauty of the Siskiyou high country, I stashed the motorcycle in the bushes where the trails ran out to hike cross country to the high ridges and, in solitude amid the flower strewn peaks, marvel at the sea of mountains on the horizon. Pretty heady stuff for a geeky kid from the plains.

The sights and smells of the Oregon high country from those days long passed, remain in my memory. The sunny days and starry nights of Southern Oregon got in my blood and I've not been able to shake them yet. Some 30 years after that sun filled summer, I found myself moving to Southern Oregon where I live today, I'm a very lucky man indeed.

Northern Oregon Backroads Guide to the PCT

MAP OF WESTERN OREGON & PCT ROUTE

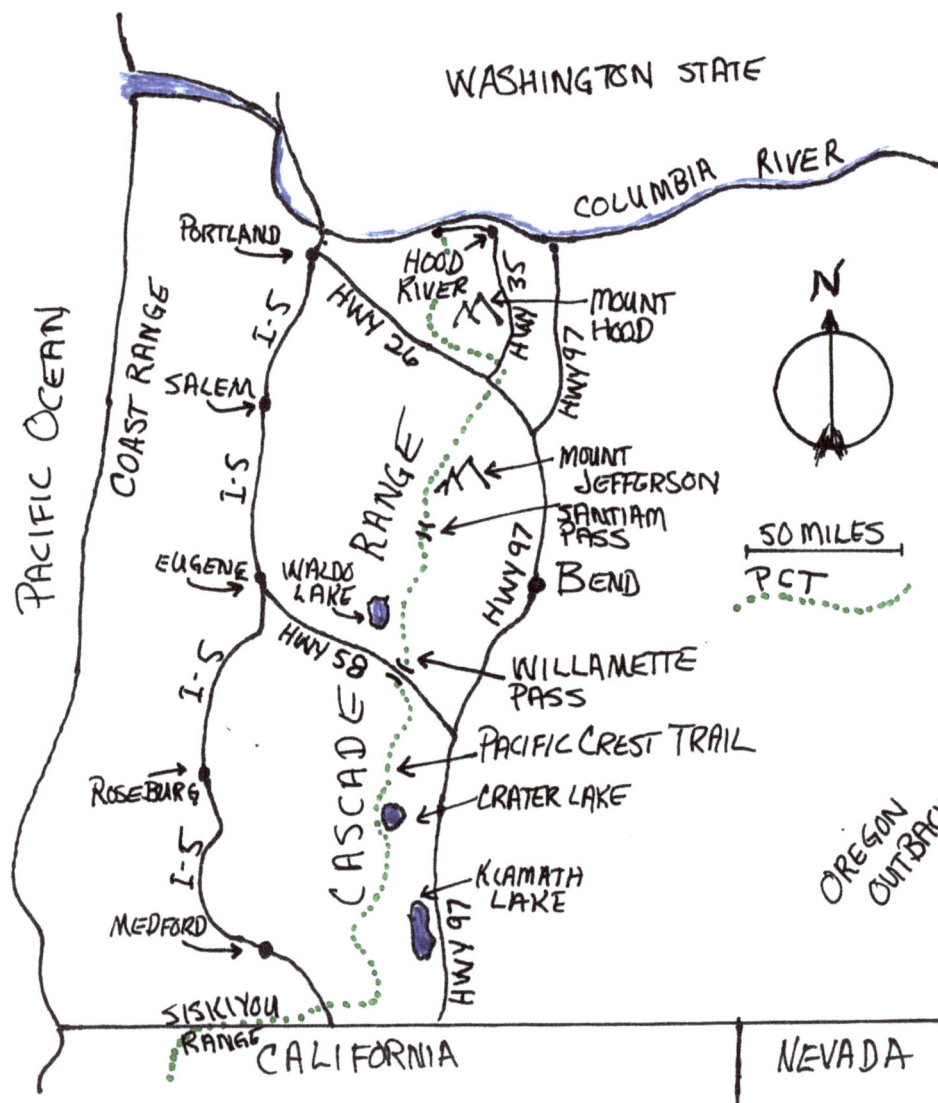

Introduction: The Twisting Journey Continues

THE LAY OF THE LAND

The high country of Oregon, California and Washington offers the chance to explore places that are still relatively wild, pristine and untrammeled. A wolf pack, founded by the famous wandering male OR-7, has taken up residence in the wilderness area surrounding southern Oregon's Mount McLoughlin, proving that given enough room, apex animals can make a living in the remaining intact roadless areas of Oregon.

Much of the road route described in this book borders on wilderness areas along Oregon's Cascade Crest. I encourage everyone to slow down and take time to get out of their car and look around the edges of this beautiful landscape, our senses are most fully tuned to the world around us at a walking speed.

From my flatlander's perspective, the high country of the Pacific Northwest has always seemed like an endless playground. Today when I find myself in the mountains, I feel moved by sun-washed high country and big skies, a place of freedom and many possibilities, including the chance of hearing wolves howling in the distance.

A campsite with a view of Broken Top Volcano. Most of the mountains in Oregon's High Cascades are geologically youngsters.

Northern Oregon Backroads Guide to the PCT

The major peaks of today's Cascades are geologically speaking, youngsters. Built during the middle Pleistocene era, few started erupting before about 700,000 years ago. The oldest lava of Mount Hood appears to approach that age. Most familiar volcanoes in the High Cascades are considerably younger than Mount Hood, with Mount Jefferson at (only) about 300,000 years old, being a trouble making punk kid.

Most of the volcanoes we see on the skyline today started to erupt around 440-450,000 thousand years ago. An earlier line of low volcanoes called the **Western Cascades**, began erupting millions of years before that and were subsequently mostly eroded away as the **High Cascades** began to rise on the rubble left behind.

The whole show is driven by the conveyer-like forces of plate tectonics as islands off the coast collided with the landmass and the heavier rocks of the Pacific Ocean are subducted below the lighter terrain making up our part of North America. Simply stated, the place beneath the land's surface where the rocks become molten drives the pyrotechnics of the Cascade volcanoes.

The Cascades are not just about fire though, long periods of time were ruled by ice. Mighty glaciers formed on the peaks and high

Some of the youngest rocks in Oregon nearly block the way near South Sister Volcano.

Introduction: The Twisting Journey Continues

ridges and may have at one time, about 18,000 years ago, formed an enormous ice cap that stretched more then 200 miles from Mount Hood in the north to Mount McLoughlin near Medford, Oregon in the south. Alpine glaciers moved down to elevations well below 3,000 feet and begin to undo these mountains built by lava rock and fire. Glacial ice extended down the mountains scooping out lakes and forming valleys in the virgin landscapes. The end of the last ice age brought the epic **Missoula Floods** that scoured the Columbia River and left deposits of silt from Montana and Washington hills layered 15 feet deep in Oregon's Willamette Valley.

Of course the eruptive phase of the upstart High Cascades is far from over as witnessed by the deadly recent (1980) eruption of Mount Saint Helens and the ongoing construction of a lava dome on that mountain's crater floor. There is evidence of extensive geologically recent eruptions and an ominous bulge along the line that forms the Three Sisters volcanoes southwest of Sisters, Oregon.

A drive to **McKenzie Pass and Dee Wright Observatory** is described in this book and highly recommended to grasp the scale of the lava fields created by the eruptions of a chain of volcanoes and vents in the surrounding area, some less than 2,000 years ago. The south side of South Sister above Devils Lake has rocks erupted as little as 1,300 years ago. Mount Hood erupted as recently as 1781, choking the Sandy and Zigzag Rivers with a mass of rocks, logs, ash and mud (known as a lahar) several feet deep.

These volcanoes are places where today we hike, ski, and camp on and around. We rely on the rivers that form on their slopes for irrigation and drinking water for millions of people. Their beauty and (seemingly) stately serenity belie their histories of violence. Now these awesome constructs of Mother Earth attract mountain lovers from around the world to explore, admire and enjoy.

THE PACIFIC CREST TRAIL

In Washington, California, and Oregon, the Pacific Crest Trail was largely cobbled together from existing routes pioneered by mountaineering groups in all three states starting in the 1920's and possibly earlier. These early north/south trails connected with existing (pre-European) foot routes that had been used by men and critters for thousands of years before that.

The **"Crest" (not coast)** part of the PCT designation means that the trail strives to follow the high country divide of river waters that flow west and directly into the Pacific Ocean from those that flow east into the Great Basin and the Gulf of California in the southern

Northern Oregon Backroads Guide to the PCT

Welcome to Oregon! Grizzled veterans of the PCT, with trail names " Messy Fruit " and "Captain Quick ," both German citizens , enter Oregon and head north at a 25 mile-per-day pace.

part of the region and the Columbia Basin in the north. In Oregon the "Skyline Trail" was constructed before the PCT existed and ran from Mount Hood to Crater Lake. Parts of this original trail still exist, some sections are paved over with modern roads, and other pieces were incorporated into today's PCT.

We can all be thankful that there were enough people of vision (and political will) to make this national treasure a reality. The Pacific Crest Trail was authorized by Congress in 1968 and dedicated in 1993; today's **PCT stretches 2,650 miles from Mexico to Canada.**

THE SCENIC ROUTE

Some time ago I started thinking about traveling the length of Oregon. Shadowing the Pacific Crest Trail I would honor Dad and seek out the scenic route.

Accompanied on many adventures by my best friend (and moderating influence) Katie Powers, I've spent the last several years compiling information and exploring some of the most beautiful country in the American West. Traveling the length of Oregon and shadowing the **Pacific Crest Trail**, we have driven the "scenic route" (thanks for the genes Dad). Taking the backroads and staying in the high country has been the mantra; keeping a journal along the way has been part of the fun too. Following the PCT from the point where it

Introduction: The Twisting Journey Continues

enters Oregon from the south (just like thru-hikers on the PCT do) all the way to the Columbia River and Washington State in the north was the ultimate goal.

I started writing *A Twisting Journey* as a way to better know this place I now call home. I suppose I can thank my parents and teachers for inspiring in me the curiosity to always seek the answer to the question: "What lies ahead?" or perhaps it's just in my blood. The question is an age old one, asked by travelers from our misty past. Many times the answer to that question may be mundane or expected, other times, exploring our world can fill us with wonder and the unexpected turns and bumps in the road are the things that stick in our memories. Perhaps the question alone is enough to make some of us want to see what's around the next corner, it seems to be enough for me.

Of course the "research" involved in exploring a **road trip version of the Pacific Crest Trail through Oregon** has meant I've had an excuse to re-live those days of youthful exploration in Oregon's mountains, this time armed with a lifetime's worth of experience and (hopefully) a little more wisdom to not only share with others but to better appreciate my surroundings on a personal level.

DON'T FORGET THE FLOATER

If you have a small boat, a car topper or inflatable, opportunities abound for floating adventures. The **canoe/kayak trail** along the northwestern shore of **Upper Klamath Lake**, described in the first book of this series, is unique and primal. The entire route passes by many lakes of significant size and several major streams. Even the first Regional description through the Southern Oregon Siskiyous has choice water features on both ends; the Applegate River and Emigrant Lake.

Ollalie Lake Scenic Area and other Regions north of Willamette Pass described in this book, stand out among many great places to explore for adventurous paddlers or those who just want to enjoy high country sun, Earth, and water. And of course there are many fishing, hiking and camping opportunities along the way as well!

Both books in this series feature an amazing assortment of glacier carved alpine lakes and streams covering Oregon's crest country, many of them out-of-the-way gems. Both books are available online, at Oregonbackroads.com, or at independent booksellers near you.

HOW TO USE THIS GUIDE

⇨ **This guide is designed to be a supplement to your maps**

Anyone who has traveled the backroads of Oregon can tell you what a challenge it can be. Many maps are lacking in detail and the traveler quickly learns after leaving the pavement that the confusing maze of roads in the real world can be different than what a map shows.

Maps already on your smartphone can be useful but may not show critical details, don't rely on them alone. Paper maps last for years without charging the battery once. I once dropped a map off a 200 foot cliff and it still worked! So paper maps are super tough too.

A Twisting Journey provides maps to help guide travelers along the general route and through key intersections. These maps are arranged starting with the Region number followed by the map number. "R" stands for Region. For example:

- Map number R5.2 would refer to Region Five, map 2
- Map number R8.1 would be Region Eight, map 1, the first map in the Region 8 series

New roads are added and old roads decommissioned. Attempts at signage over time come and go. Signs sometimes are flat out lies, missing , or SUBAR (Shot Up Beyond All Recognition). Some key intersections and general routes for each region are sketched out for clarity but take a map too! As any good guide should be, this is definitely a work in progress. I have attempted to be as accurate as possible but know my efforts fall well short of perfection. I would ask the readers and users of this work to contact me with suggestions and corrections at ewmcb40@gmail.com

BE PREPARED! (Wisdom from an old Boy Scout)

A word about safety and etiquette when traveling the backroads:

- Consider the season and the weather when planning a trip in the high country.
- Inquire locally before traveling through snow country. Contact local Ranger Stations, for information on local road conditions.
- Some storms can dump several feet of snow in a single blast, and then the weather may turn off dry and sunny for weeks at a time. It's not unusual to see several feet of snow on the ground at any time in the late fall through early spring at high elevations in the Siskiyous and Cascades. It also hasn't been unusual in some recent years to see nothing on the ground in January followed by

Introduction: The Twisting Journey Continues

heavy snows through the spring months.

- Pay attention to the weather and you'll sometimes find the most beautiful days in the mountains can be in January or February. This is especially true when the typical wintertime high pressure temperature inversions trap colder air and pollutants in the valleys below, leaving the higher terrain sunny and warm.
- Be careful with fire! Things can be critically dry in the mountains of Oregon during the summer and fall. A bucket and shovel are a good idea. Don't ignore fire restrictions and only start campfires in existing fire rings.
- Practice good etiquette. Traveling as lightly as possible across the land should be our goal.
- This means leaving a minimum footprint. Much of this route is through high country with thin soils and short growing seasons. Avoid driving off established roads and respect wetlands. Please be sure to pick up your own trash and pitch in to pick up after those less considerate.
- Fill your gas tank where you can! Just do it.
- Plan to use more fuel per mile on back roads. Your vehicle works at consistently lower gears because you're at altitude and going slower. When traveling off the beaten path, gas stations and grocery stores can be few and far between. A full gas tank is peace of mind, right?
- Allow extra time. Create the opportunity to stop and smell the wildflowers.
- Most regional routes described in this book are less than one hundred miles and can be driven (rushed through) in less time than the Guide recommends. However, much of the way is along roads that are less than perfect so expect to travel more slowly.
- Obtain maps of the area. This guide references Forest Service maps found at your friendly Ranger Station, but look for maps on-line too.
- Despite the paucity of cellphone coverage in many of the areas described in this book, **very useful apps** for navigating while off-line are available **for your smartphone**. Hikers on the PCT have a couple of free apps that they depend on to navigate the trail. Once the desired maps are loaded on your device you are independent of the internet.

Northern Oregon Backroads Guide to the PCT

- Another useful map set for paper map freaks is the *"Oregon Road and Recreation Atlas"* published by Benchmark Maps and available at your local outdoor goods retailer. This has the entire set of Oregon maps laid out in logical fashion along with tons of useful general information.
- Blankets /Sleeping Bags/Warm Clothes. Yes even in the summer. The high country is, well...high, and that means changeable weather and potential for cold temps any time of the year. Bring water and food, one gallon per person/beast per day is a good idea.

OTHER ITEMS TO CONSIDER

This is the part of the book that gets dry and most people skip through this boring crap to get to the maps and descriptions so I'm just gonna throw all of this stuff into a big old heap-o-words and like a yard sale, let you pick through it for anything you may find useful. I'm assuming everyone has that thang called common sense so there's really no need to mention all of this stuff anyway, right?

First Aid Kit, Flashlight and Batteries, Matches/Lighter/Candle, Knife Hatchet/Ax/Folding Saw, Spade Tip Shovel (the most useful shape for most purposes), Jumper Cables/Spare Ignition Key, Chains during snow season, Small Tarp and at least 50 feet of Stout Rope, Sun Block, Insect Repellent, Toilet Paper, Folding Chairs (for bird watching, bulls*#*!ing, and beer drinking).

Do you need all this stuff? Probably not, but just like flood insurance, that day when the water started rushing into your house, it was all worth it. It's at least a good idea to keep some of these items in a large duffel bag, ready to toss in the car year 'round.

BAD FEELINGS

⇨ **If you ever get one of these gut feelings, stop and listen to your visceral self. Don't freak out, assess your options. Turn back if you have serious doubts. Is the snow piling up and the hour getting late? Don't hesitate to turn around before the snow gets too deep to do so easily.**

Certain all wheel drive vehicles (like a Subaru Outback) have just enough clearance and traction to get your ass into serious trouble when it becomes high centered in the snow. Your big snarly SUV/pick- up (like a Toyota Tundra) can often travel even further up the mountain before high centering, so let's not be smug, eh?

Sometimes though, trouble comes in other forms. For instance,

Introduction: The Twisting Journey Continues

Make sure to carefully consider your vehicle when choosing a route. A four-wheel-drive with high clearance is necessary for some places.

is your spare tire inflated? I'm not even going to ask if you have a jack and tire wrench… Another good way to get yourself in trouble is relying on your GPS (Global Positioning System). Although these devices are becoming more sophisticated, some serious high profile mishaps involving lost families have forced manufacturers to be more careful with "shortcut directions".

Google maps supplied with most smart phones today are remarkably accurate on the larger scale, but don't glue your eyes to the little blue dot while you drive off the cliff, OK?

Off the beaten path your smartphone is definitely useful where you can get reception (or the battery isn't dead), but don't rely on that alone. **Download off-line map apps for your smart phone**.

The best problem solving device you have is your brain. It's also the best tool for staying out of trouble to begin with. Please be safe, pay attention, be kind to each other and don't drop your keys in the river.

A FEW WORDS ABOUT VEHICLES

With the exception of Region Nine (Government Camp to Bridge of the Gods), all road route descriptions have short stretches of rough road, not advised for low clearance, two-wheel drive vehicles. I'm not saying you can't avoid the worst of the rocks and ruts in your '03 Chevy Impala to make it through the entire backroads route from

Northern Oregon Backroads Guide to the PCT

Ollalie Lake is one of many high lakes we'll explore. Cloud shrouded Mount Jefferson frames the horizon.

Willamette Pass to The Columbia River, just saying I don't advise it for the sections of rough road described.

The majority of this route is paved or improved gravel and can be done safely in any vehicle with a normal wheelbase and reasonable clearance in good weather. Where clearance and traction are an issue I have tried to provide **alternate routes for those of us who like our low ridin' rigs**.

Certain all wheel drive vehicles (like a Subaru Outback) have just enough clearance and traction to get your ass in serious trouble when it becomes high centered in the snow. Your big snarly SUV/pick- up (like a Toyota Tundra) can often travel even further up the mountain before high centering, so let's not be smug, eh?

Of course traveling as lightly as possible has its virtues beyond better gas mileage and a shorter turning radius. A smaller passenger car (a Toyota Camry for reference) has greater range and overall leaves a smaller footprint on the land but may have clearance and traction issues on rougher roads. All of the paved roads and most of the gravel roads described in this guide are perfectly suited to this vehicle in good weather.

Other short wheelbase, two-wheel drive vehicles (let's call it a Ford Ranger pick-up) can often go places where a passenger car can't. In the back country, clearance is usually more of an issue than traction in good weather.

Introduction: The Twisting Journey Continues

The other vehicle in the mix is the new generation of midsize SUVs with all-wheel drive. This type of vehicle (like a Subaru Outback) is a nice compromise between clearance, maneuverability, gas mileage, and traction but a little tight for two or three people and a dog.

Your big snarly/gas hoggy, four-wheel-drive SUV or pick-up (let's call it a Lincoln Navigator) has lots of room for the family and gear and has all the clearance and traction you'll probably ever need to ford a river or scale a mountain (but when was the last time you needed to do that?). Jeep type four-wheel-drive vehicles are made to travel the backroads and needless to say, in good weather, none of the road descriptions contained within this guide are beyond the capabilities of such vehicles.

As I've poked and prodded around the cracks and crannies of the mountains of the west, I've felt a growing connection with this ever changing land and my place in it. There are so many places left to explore, I doubt if this one lifetime will be long enough to ever see it all, so let's get crackin'!

Slow down, take a look around. Explore. Enjoy the day, and wave (at least lift your little finger off the steering wheel) to your fellow travelers!

The freedom of the hills calls to me.
And so I must go.   Ed W. McBee

Wildly beautiful Lady's Slipper Orchids (Cypripediodeae) can be found in open woodlands near Mount Hood.

MULTI-REGION MAP 1: REGIONS 5, 6, & 7

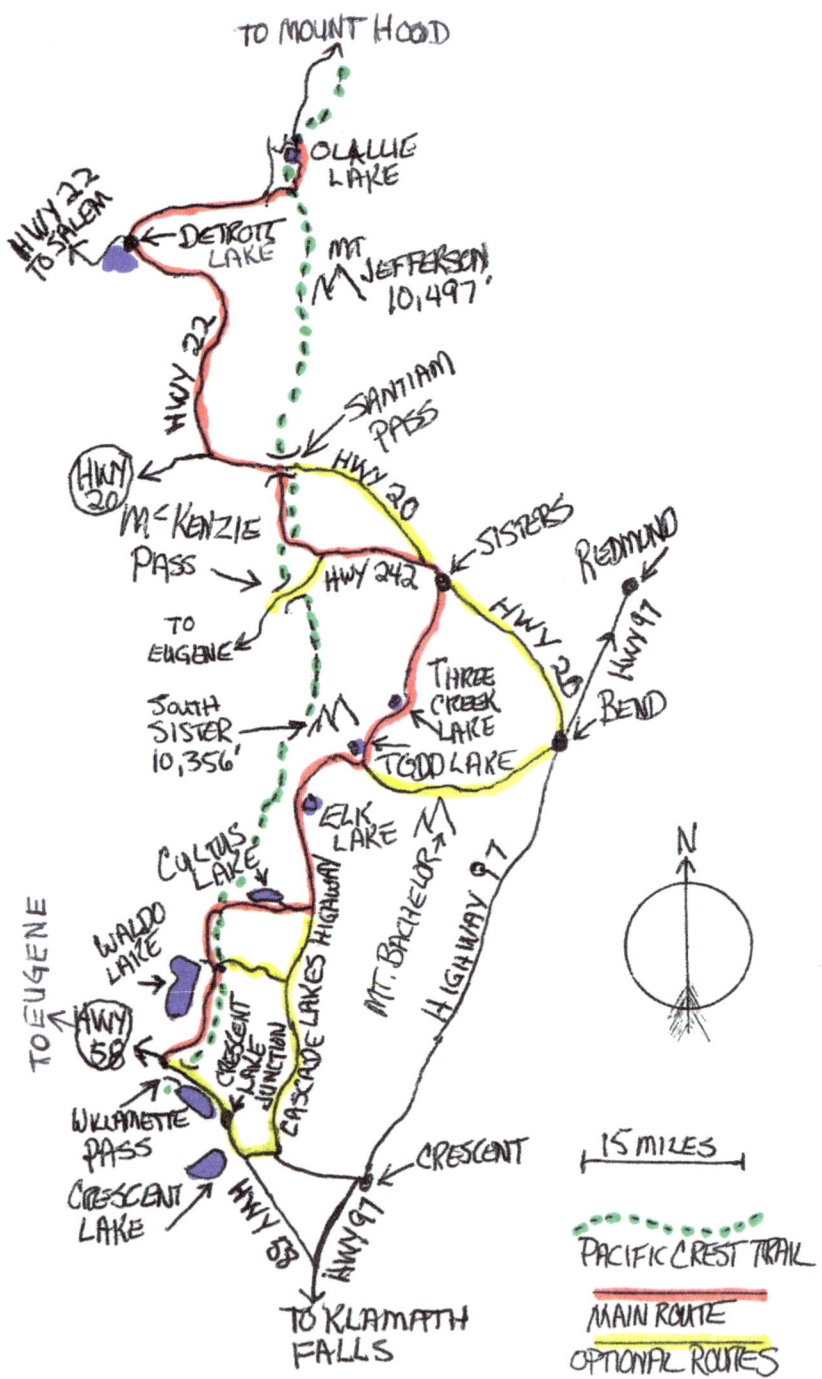

REGION FIVE
Willamette Pass to Elk Lake

Adventure awaits paddlers on Region Five's Taylor Lake.

"Touch the Earth, love the Earth, and honor the Earth,
Her plains, her valleys, her hills and her seas;
Rest your spirit in her solitary places
For the gifts of life are the Earth's and
they are given to all."

— *Henry Beston*

Region 5 — Willamette Pass to Elk Lake

ROUTE DESCRIPTION

Do you like high mountain lakes? Mountain lake lovers will salivate over the variety of beautiful Oregon high country water in Region Five. The Region Five Main Route begins at **Willamette Pass**. After exploring Odell Lake, we'll travel west on Highway 58 for 3.3 miles to the **Waldo Lake Road** where we'll turn north and traverse the east side of sparkling **Waldo Lake** to the North Waldo Campground.

The **primitive Irish and Taylor Lakes – 514 Road** heads north from the campground entrance and after turning east, crosses the Cascade Crest into eastern Oregon before encountering the **Pacific Crest Trail** along Forest Road 4636. We'll explore isolated **Irish and Taylor Lakes** and a couple of trout lakes along the Many Lakes Trail. Little Cultus Lake Campground begins our exploration of the **Cascade Lakes** country. After turning north on the **Cascade Lakes Highway**, Region Five ends at **Elk Lake**, west of Mount Bachelor.

ROAD CONDITIONS

Drive the **Optional Roads** (marked in Yellow on the **Guide Map**) **to avoid the primitive roads connecting Waldo Lake** with **Little Cultus Campground** and **Cascade Lakes Highway / Road 46**.

⇨ **Special Note:** *By all means visit peaceful **Charlton Lake** at the beginning of the optional 4290 Road (near Waldo Lake), regardless of your chosen route north or the vehicle you're driving. The **Pacific Crest Trail** skirts the west side of Charlton Lake and crosses the 4290 road near the lake.*

For those choosing to take one of the two optional roads from Waldo Lake, I recommend backtracking down the Waldo Lake Road to Willamette Pass and Highway 58. From Willamette Pass, drive 9 miles east on Highway 58 to the Crescent Cut-Off Road. Proceed three miles northeast on the Cut-Off Road to the first junction, turn left, and follow the signs for the Cascade Lakes Highway / Road 46.

The paved Cascade Lakes Highway (described below) has become world famous for its beauty, and rightly so. Beginning at Davis Lake and ascending to the Mount Bachelor Ski Area, County Road 46 takes the traveler through some breathtaking country featuring ice-carved volcanoes, luscious meadows, ice-cold lakes, lava

⇦ *Salt Creek Falls are near Willamette Pass, the start of Region Five.*

Northern Oregon Backroads Guide to the PCT

fields, and sparkling streams. This high country wonderland attracts hoards of visitors from nearby Bend, Oregon's fastest growing city, and other visitors from around the world. For those who want to learn more about the area, take the time to stop and read the many informational signs along the highway.

The **other option from Waldo Lake** is to drive the 4290 Road east (about 8 miles) past Charlton Lake, hooking up with the Cascade Lakes Highway near Crane Prairie Reservoir. It looks tempting on the map to take this short-cut and normally, in the spirit of the *Backroads Guide*, I'd say go ahead. There are two signs at the beginning of the road, one indicating eight miles to the Century Drive, the other advising the driver that this is an unimproved road. Only 8 miles, how bad can it be, right?

Granted, the 4290 Road is superior to the Irish and Taylor / 514 Road, and if there were some little thing, a pleasant creek, an inspiring viewpoint, something that makes this rocky, dusty, road worthwhile, I'd go for it. Maybe I'm missing something, but this route offers little more than a pounding. With care you can drive any vehicle on the 4290 Road, but unless you're driving a Baja 1000-ready vehicle or a dirt-bike, it'll take about the same amount of time to drive around

PCT hikers at Shelter Cove share a beer. The hiker on the left displays a bandaged foot.

Region 5 — Willamette Pass to Elk Lake

MAP R5.1: WILLAMETTE PASS TO ELK LAKE

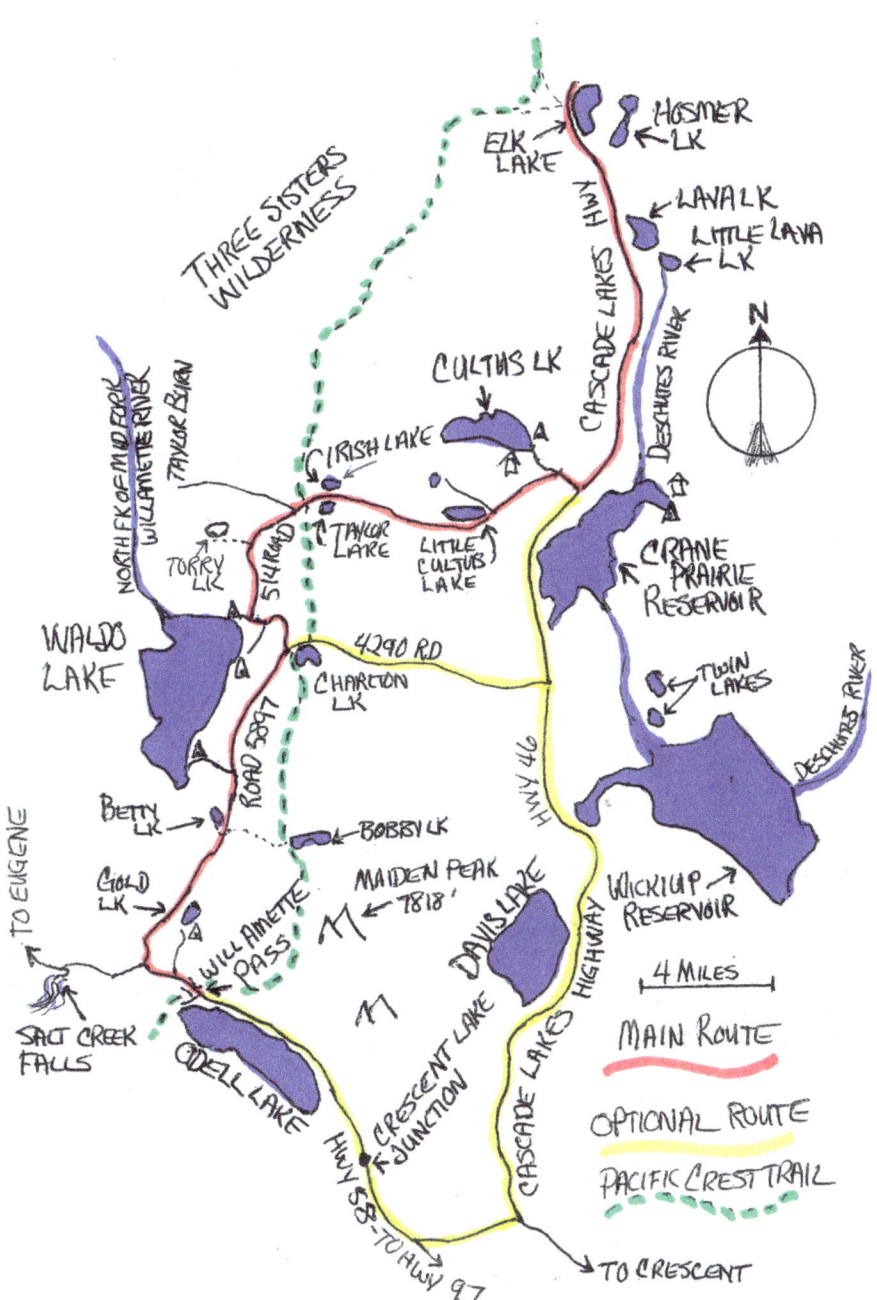

Northern Oregon Backroads Guide to the PCT

(about one hour via Highway 58) as it does to drive this monotonous 8 miles of rough track at (an optimistic) 8 miles per hour. Your call...

Charlton Lake Trailhead lies less than a quarter-mile from the Waldo Lake Road, and the **Pacific Crest Trail** crosses the 4290 Road a very short way past the trailhead. Possible campsites for tent campers and smaller RVs are adjacent to the trailhead to the lake.

PACIFIC CREST TRAIL ACCESS POINTS
Four access points to the Pacific Crest Trail are in Region Five:

1. The Pacific Crest Trailhead at **Willamette Pass** is near the ski resort turn-in and the beginning of Region Five.

2. The next road access for hikers heading north from the pass is at the **Charlton Lake / 4290 Road**, about 15 trail miles from Willamette Pass.

3. The next road crossing for hikers northbound on the PCT is at the **Irish and Taylor Lakes / 4636 Road**, about 22 trail miles from Willamette Pass.

4. From Irish and Taylor Lakes, it's about thirteen trail miles to the **short access trail to Elk Lake**, the Cascade Lakes Highway and the end of Region Five.

South from Willamette Pass on the PCT to Summit Lake / 6010 Road near Summit Lake Campground is about 21 trail miles (described in the companion volume to this guide).

A Twisting Journey: Southern Oregon Backroads Guide to the PCT covers road connections to the PCT in southern Oregon. Spanning the state of Oregon from the point the PCT enters Oregon (California state line) to the Willamette Pass, it is the companion guide to this book.

MAPS FOR REGION FIVE
- Benchmark Maps – *Oregon Road and Recreation Atlas* – pages 73 and 74
- *Deschutes National Forest Visitors Map*

For Willamette National Forest road information call the Middle Fork Ranger District near Oakridge: 541-782-2283. For information in the Deschutes National Forest call the Ranger Station in Crescent at 541-433-3200 or the District Headquarters in Bend at 541-383-5300.

Region 5 — Willamette Pass to Elk Lake

MAIN ROADS IN ORDER OF TRAVEL

All Regional Routes are described South to North.

State Highway 58	This is the paved Willamette Pass Highway
Waldo Lake / Road 5897	This paved road takes us north and becomes the 5898 Road at the Charlton Lake Junction.
North Waldo Campground / Road 5898	After leaving the Charlton Lake Junction this paved road leads to North Waldo Campground and the beginning of the 514 Road.
Forest Road 514 / Irish and Taylor Road	This primitive dirt road leads north from the entrance of North Waldo Campground to an intersection with the Taylor Burn / Irish and Taylor Road.
Forest Road 4636	After leaving the Taylor Burn intersection this road heads east past Irish and Taylor Lakes and ultimately to the stop sign at the 4635 Road near Cultus Lake.
Cultus Lake Road / Road 4635	Turn left (west) and this paved road leads to Cultus Lake Resort and the adjacent campground. The Main Route turns right (east) to the Cascade Lakes Highway.
Cascade Lakes Highway / County Road 46	We'll head north for 12 miles along this paved highway to Elk Lake and the end of Region Five.

Northern Oregon Backroads Guide to the PCT

OPTIONAL ROADS & SECONDARY ROADS

Forest Road 4290	This is the rough, dusty, and featureless optional road from North Waldo Lake to the Cascade Lakes Highway.
Highway 58 east from Willamette Pass	This is the other (preferred in my opinion) optional road from North Waldo. It involves backtracking down the Waldo Lake Road but avoids the rough and monotonous 4290 Road.
Gold Lake Road	The Gold Lake Road is slightly more than a mile west of Willamette Pass and leads to the Marilyn Lakes Trailhead and Gold Lake Campground. This is a dead-end road.
Crescent Cut-Off Road	The Cut-Off Road intersection is about 3 miles east of the town of Crescent Lake Junction.
Cascade Lakes Highway north to Cultus Lake	After we turn left from the Cut-Off Road we'll pass Davis Lake, Wickiup Reservoir, and Crane Prairie Reservoir before rejoining the Main Route at Cultus Lake Road.

⇨ **Special Note:** *The road to **Odell Butte Lookout** lies further east along Highway 58, another 2.4 miles from the Crescent Cut-Off Road. The 5815 Road ascends Odell Butte in a series of switchbacks about 6 miles to a gate. Walk another 0.7 miles to the lookout cabin and some amazing vistas of the region. Bring water and your camera; on a clear day the views are a hundred miles in every direction. Grab your map to help identify the many local lakes and peaks visible from the observation deck. The lookout is manned during the fire season and is open to the public during daylight hours.*

Region 5 — Willamette Pass to Elk Lake

From the road to Odell Butte Lookout, Crescent Lake lies at the foot of Diamond Peak in the distance.

ROAD NOTES — REGION FIVE

Starting at Willamette pass, the following notes give details about the sights, history, and attractions along the way.

<u>**WILLAMETTE PASS AREA:**</u> Elevation 5,126 ft.
(Pronounced: wil-LAM-mit)

Okay, I'll get this off my chest first, and then we can move on. What we know today as Willamette Pass would be more properly named **Salt Creek Pass**. Salt Creek, beginning at nearby Gold Lake, is a beautiful stream and a major contributor to the Middle Fork Willamette River where it merges near the town of Oakridge.

The "real" Willamette Pass is about 10 miles south of here. **Emigrant Pass** near Summit Lake (described in the Southern Oregon companion volume to this book), is much closer to the headwaters of the Middle Fork Willamette at Lake Timpanogas. "Salt" Creek was perhaps considered bad PR for a newly developed wagon road. Since many of the settlers streaming into Oregon after the Civil War ended in 1865 had already heard of the fabled Willamette Valley, so much the better and the Willamette Pass name stuck.

★ 25 ★

Northern Oregon Backroads Guide to the PCT

The railroad uses a low-spot (tunnel) in the Cascades less than a mile south of Willamette Pass Highway, calling the rail gap **"Pengra" Pass** just to muddy the pass-naming waters, I guess. For hikers heading north, The **Pacific Crest Trail** crosses Pengra Pass before crossing Highway 58 at (so-called) Willamette Pass.

Whew…Okay, I feel better now.

The **Ski Area at Willamette Pass** is open on a limited basis in the summer. On weekends, the lifts take hikers to the summit of twin-topped Eagle Peak, elevation 6,683 feet. Hike from there back to the parking lot at 5,120 feet. and lose 1,563 feet. elevation. The wildflower show begins in July and lasts into September on these high Cascade ridges. Contact the resort for information:

Willamette Pass Ski Resort
541-345-7668

Optional Salt Creek Falls: Look for the turn-off to the falls viewing area about a mile west (towards Oakridge) beyond the Waldo Lake turn-off on Highway 58.

Salt Creek Falls is **Oregon's second highest plunge falls** (after Multnomah Falls) and a spectacular sight. The viewing area has an informational kiosk and a trail that wraps around the edge of the basalt ledge forming the falls. Created by the usual combination of Cascade fire (volcanoes) and ice (glaciers), the falls thunder over a 286-foot drop to the splash pool below. The road to the parking area is not plowed, and it's usually gated after the first heavy snow of the year. If the gate is closed and the snow isn't too deep, walk about 0.4 miles to the falls viewing area from the gate. Afternoon light is best for photography.

ODELL LAKE AREA

Odell Lake is one of the largest natural lakes in the Cascades. The lake offers a number of camping and resort options.

CAMPSITES IN THE ODELL LAKE AREA

Four drive-in campgrounds and one boat-in campground are on Odell Lake.

Trapper Creek Campground: Located adjacent to the resort on the west end of Odell, Trapper Creek Campground is a pleasant and sheltered spot from the wind and wave action kicked up on the big lake. An easy trail connects the campground to Shelter Cove Resort

Region 5 — Willamette Pass to Elk Lake

The boat launch at Trapper Creek features a view of the Willamette Pass Ski Area.

along the point formed by the small peninsula upon which both the campground and resort reside.

Trapper Creek is a major contributor to Odell Lake and a major spawning creek for the lake's kokanee (landlocked salmon) in the fall. Bald eagles can be seen in the trees and along the streams when the fish are in their spawning colors. The Trapper Creek Campground and the grounds around the resort are a great spot to observe these powerful birds in considerable numbers as they prey upon the love-crazy fish.

Across the road from the entrance to the campground is a trailhead with interpretive signs naming the trees along the riparian area. This is also a great place to look for wildflowers in the spring and summer. The campground has a boat launch and 32 campsites, some of which can accommodate trailers to 40 feet.

Princess Creek Campground: Located on the north side of Odell Lake with big views to the south of Diamond Peak, Princess Creek has two docks adjacent to the boat launch. The campground has water, handicap accessible toilets, and 46 fee sites, some which can accommodate trailers to 50 feet. The large day-use area is east of the boat landing with a sunny southern exposure. This is another beach

Northern Oregon Backroads Guide to the PCT

where the wind is reliable in the afternoons and wind jockeys can show off their stuff.

Sunset Cove Campground: This camp is located on the south side of Highway 58 amid the towering trees. There's a boat launch at adjacent Chinquapin Point with a fish cleaning station. The day-use area is promoted as a place for the wind surfing crowd, separate from the boat launch. It's $5 to use the day-use area. The boat launch is sheltered by a rock jetty with a walkway to the end of it. Sunset has 24 fee sites and wheelchair accessible facilities.

Odell Creek Campground: Located on the east end of the lake adjacent to Odell Lake Lodge, Odell Creek Campground has 30 fee sites with several waterfront sites. A couple of the campsites are located on two small peninsulas with water on virtually three sides. A boat launch and drinking water are available, and with the resort close by, a restaurant and store too!

Pebble Bay Campground: This campground is a boat-in site with two official campsites and other informal sites along the southern shore of the lake. The campground is about 1.5 water miles east from Shelter Cove Resort.

ODELL LAKE RESORTS

Depending on your style, you can choose between two resorts that offer accommodations at Odell Lake.

Odell Lake Lodge
541-433-2540

Odell Lake Lodge is the friendly "Grandfather" of Oregon lake resorts. Located on the eastern shore of big, glacier-carved Odell Lake, the resort was founded in 1902. This is apparently the oldest of the mountain lake resorts in Oregon. The large marina is situated next to where Odell Creek begins its journey to the Deschutes River. The marina rents power boats and offers guided fishing trips during the season. They also rent canoes, kayaks, and paddleboats. The dog-friendly resort offers cabins for rent year-round.

During the winter, this is ground zero for the cross-country ski crowd with many miles of trails at your doorstep. Skis, snowshoes, and sleds are available for rent after the snow flies. The lodge has a restaurant (that serves excellent food) and an attractive patio overlooking the creek and the marina. On summer weekends the lodge hosts live music on the outdoor patio.

Region 5 — Willamette Pass to Elk Lake

Sunset Cove has a rock Jetty with a sidewalk to the end.

The cabins are on the glacial ridge above the lake, many with magnificent views. For those seeking peace and quiet, request cabin #17, the one at the end of the resort road.

Shelter Cove Resort
541-433-2548

Shelter Cove Resort, located on the west end of Odell Lake, is one-stop shopping for hikers on the Pacific Crest Trail, fishermen (and fisherwomen), skiers, and other winter enthusiasts and those just seeking solace during the off season.

When word gets out that fishing for kokanee is hot, boats line the docks at Shelter Cove (around mid-June most years). The fish cleaning table at midday is cheek to jowl with customers cleaning the tasty fish.

Located just east of the Cascade Crest, Shelter Cove lures hikers off the trail to re-supply and maybe rent a cabin for the night. The store has the usual camper's needs along with an array of fishing tackle. Besides espressos and snacks, the store has quite a selection of clothes from t-shirts to jackets. The fire is regularly stoked in the outside fire-pit along the path to the marina. There is no restaurant or bar.

Northern Oregon Backroads Guide to the PCT

Boats line the docks in front of the fish cleaning station at Shelter Cove Resort.

The resort rents eight housekeeping cabins along with more luxurious accommodations in the "Kokanee Lodge." There's fuel for your boat at the marina but no auto fuel. The marina is large and even has space for those who wish to sleep aboard their boats. The boat launch is available to the public for a $5 fee. The resort also offers RV spaces and tent camping sites.

During the winter, Shelter Cove has discounted rates on lodging and rents snowshoes and cross country skis. The ski area at Willamette Pass is a short drive from the resort.

GOLD LAKE ROAD: Elevation 5,030 ft.

> ⇨ **Special note:** *On some large-scale maps it looks like the Gold Lake Road intersects the Waldo Lake Road at Gold Lake Campground. Gold Lake Road is a dead-end and is gated at Highway 58 after the snow flies.*

It's about three miles to the campground on an easy gravel road from Highway 58. The road is narrow in spots with some pot-holes and muddy spots early in the season but suitable for campers, small trailers, and passenger cars.

Marilyn Lakes Trail: About half-way to Gold Lake, **look for a trailhead** on your left to Marilyn Lakes. There are no signs but a

Region 5 — Willamette Pass to Elk Lake

MAP R5.2: WALDO LAKE & OPTIONAL 4290 ROAD

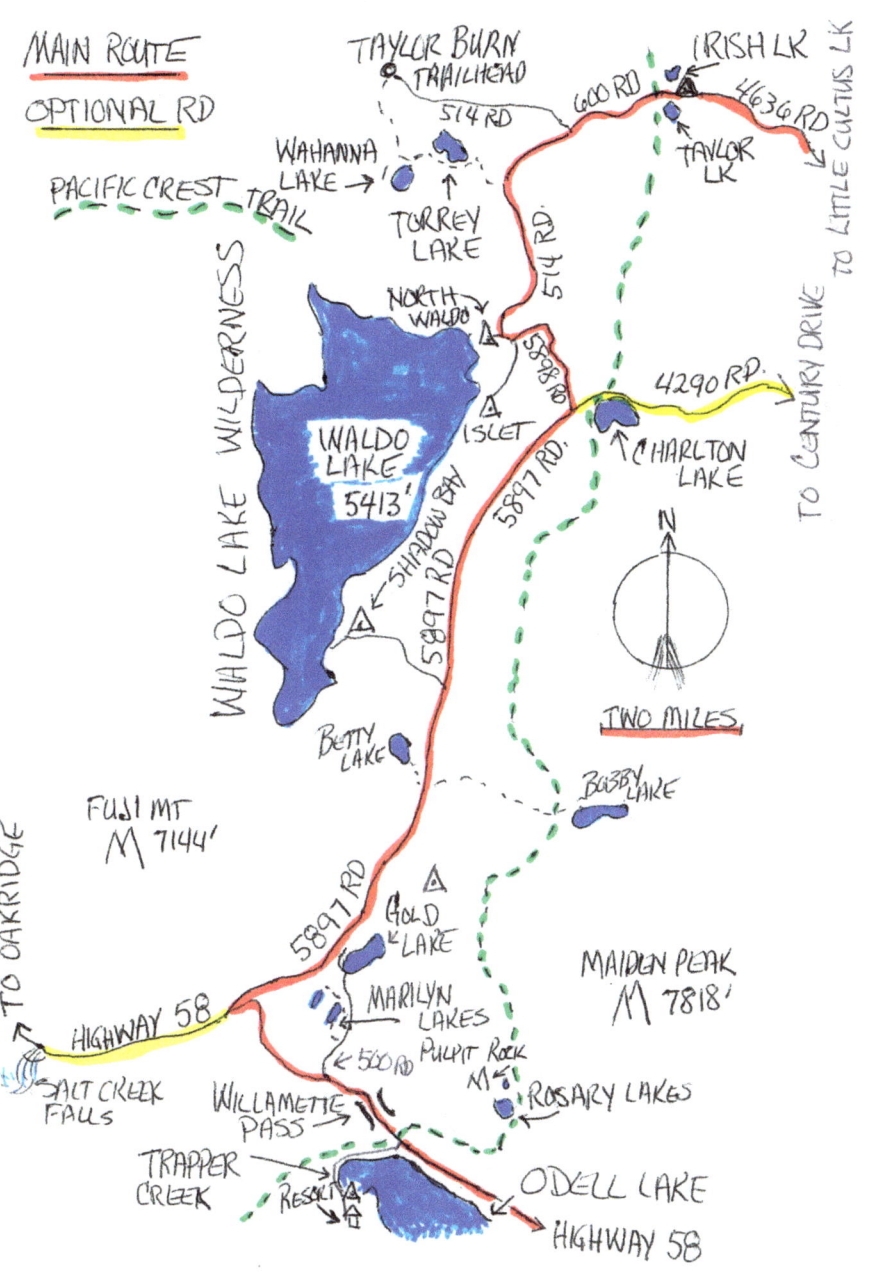

small parking area marks the trail. The path heads downhill and shortly arrives (less than 0.5 mi.) at Upper Marilyn Lake. A camp spot is here among the huckleberries and the big trees. The trail continues around the north side of the lake to Lower Marilyn Lake and another campsite for backpackers. Each of the Marilyns is about 20 acres and hold some nice brook trout. A float tube and fly rod are the best way to fish these lakes, with fall probably the best time to fish. Fly fishermen usually head to nearby Gold Lake to test their skills so these two lakes only receive light pressure during the year.

Gold Lake Campground: Located on the south side of the lake where Salt Creek originates, this campground is popular with the fly fishing crowd and offers some good fishing for rainbow and brook trout. Fishing is restricted to fly angling and barbless hooks. After the late spring or early summer ice-off, fishermen show up here in fair numbers. During the summer season when fishing dies off, the campground is very quiet and a great spot for paddlers and those seeking a more laid-back camping experience. Fishing picks up somewhat in the fall.

After crossing the road bridge, there are a couple of more campsites and a **trailhead** at the road's end, marked by a vault toilet and a turn-around. The trail heads north from the campground and soon forks. The trail heading north stays high above the lake with no easy access to the water near the trailhead. The fork heading west arrives at the Waldo Lake Road in only a quarter mile.

WALDO LAKE ROAD: Elevation 4,408 ft.

From Highway 58 we head to North Waldo Campground on Waldo Lake Road. From the Highway 58 intersection, Waldo Lake Road is paved and heads north. It's a good road and takes us steadily uphill. Keep an eye to the right for a small turn-out about two miles from Highway 58, where some signs high in the trees mark the **trail to Gold Lake**. The trail from Waldo Lake Road to Gold Lake Campground (see above) is about quarter-mile long.

Back on the Waldo Road we head uphill another 3.5 miles to the large parking area on the left marking the Betty Lake Trailhead.

The circle tree at Betty Lake is a nice place to take in the view.

Betty Lake Trailhead: Elevation 5,540 ft.

Sounding vaguely like a Hollywood starlet from the 1930s or '40s (maybe a cross between Betty Grable and Veronica Lake?), Betty Lake is a quarter-mile hike from the Waldo Road. The trailhead parking lot is big enough to park a dozen semis so it's hard to miss on your left as you ascend towards Waldo Lake. Another smaller lake is a stone's throw below the south end of the parking lot with a boot-beaten path down to it. Across the highway is the trail to Betty's less social sibling, **Bobby Lake** (about a 5-mile hike round-trip).

The trail to Betty Lake (elevation 5,580 ft.) is slightly uphill and crosses a creek before arriving at the lake. The lake is visible through the trees to your left at the first trail fork and leads to the mysterious "Circle Tree" of Betty Lake. Twisted by forces unknown (Druids?), this survivor tree grows in an almost 300-degree circle and is at seat height. Just past the mysterious tree, the path leads through the woods to a campsite on the lake's shoreline.

Follow the path around the south side of the lake and you'll find a peninsula connecting the shore to a nice pack-in campsite with a tiny, sheltered cove. The lake covers about 35 to 40 acres and produces some nice rainbow to 20 inches or more. It's close enough to the road to pack your inflatable boat for easier fishing access.

The main trail past the east side of Betty Lake leads to three small lakes, Howkum (as in: "How come we went this way, Dad?") and the others appropriately named Tiny and Horsefly Lakes, before joining up with the **Waldo Lake Trail** or road access to Shadow Bay Campground.

WALDO LAKE CAMPGROUNDS

Three campgrounds are available in the Waldo Lake area.

Shadow Bay: This big campground with 92 sites is located on the southeast side of the lake. A boat launch and day-use area with some campsites are located on rocky promontories. The campground is improved with water and vault toilets.

You've probably seen Idaho's license plates that say "Famous Potatoes?" Perhaps a good motto for Waldo Lake might be thus: "Waldo Lake, Famous Mosquitoes." Because of the famous mosquitoes that fill the air in June and July, many campsites are usually available until the middle of August when the skeeterfest is (mostly) over and humans can again bare un-DEET'ed flesh.

Region 5 — Willamette Pass to Elk Lake

September often turns on warm and dry with nary a sign of the winged devils.

A brief foray to Waldo in July is still a good time if you don't mind the thirsty skeeters buzzing your face and looking for any chink in your chemical armor while you're onshore. The bugs are worst during the late afternoon and evening hours. DEET really does work (35% DEET is more effective than 100%) and keeps you from being bitten but it doesn't stop the annoying buzzing and in-your-face aerobatics.

Mosquitoes, like all plants and animals in the wild, have their good years and bad years. Recent drought conditions in much of the west have probably reduced mosquito numbers in some areas. Early season hiking and camping conditions in 2019 featured dry and warm weather, less snow than average in the southern part of the Cascade Range (with the southern Oregon Siskiyous being severely impacted by low snow conditions), and fewer mosquitoes than this writer has seen in memory. So…don't let the "Famous Mosquitoes" scare you off, go prepared, wear britches and long-sleeved shirts, and don't forget the head nets and the DEET; you and your buzzing friends will have the place mostly to yourselves.

If you have a boat, you can escape the wee bloodsuckers on the water; mosquitoes don't seem to fly more than a few hundred feet from shore. Sleeping adrift on an air mattress upon Waldo Lake suddenly becomes something the blood-depleted camper may wish to consider.

North Waldo Campground: North Waldo Campground is a popular place to camp for the non-motorized boat crowd. There are also many opportunities to mountain bike and hike the trails in this relatively flat terrain.

> ⇨ **Special Note:** *The 514/Irish and Taylor Lakes Road heads north from the North Waldo Campground entrance.*

Fishing in Waldo is mostly a waste of time (time well wasted perhaps) because the big, spring-fed lake is mostly devoid of algae and the accompanying food chain to support large populations of fish. These conditions make the water incredibly clear and clean with the bottom plainly visible at depths far exceeding 90 feet on calm days. **Waldo Lake is among the clearest bodies of water in the world.**

Northern Oregon Backroads Guide to the PCT

The crystal waters of Waldo lake lure paddlers and sailors.

A large boat ramp is located next door to the campground and just north of the ramp is a sheltered day-use beach and swimming area. A few picnic tables are on shore and a floating platform is anchored just offshore for swimmers. **No motors are allowed on Waldo Lake.**

North Waldo is a good place to headquarter for hiking and exploring the many lakes in the **Waldo Lake Wilderness** or hiking the **Waldo Lake Trail**. For those who choose to hike (or jog) around **Oregon's second largest natural lake** (after Upper Klamath Lake), the trail is about 22 miles and can be done in a day or less by the aerobically fit, but usually is a two-day backpack.

Several unimproved boat-in campsites are located around the lake for those launching at any of the three campgrounds. Hiking trails abound with several trails to hike-in lakes branching off the Waldo Trail. **Waldo Lake is the headwater of the North Fork of the Middle Fork Willamette River.** The river flows from the northwest side of the lake and joins the Middle Willamette several miles to the west, near Oakridge.

Islet Point Campground: Islet Point lies to the south of North Waldo Campground. A bit smaller, it's otherwise a near mirror image of North Waldo Campground with the same amenities.

Region 5 — Willamette Pass to Elk Lake

MAP R5.3: CHARLETON LAKE TO LITTLE CULTUS LAKE

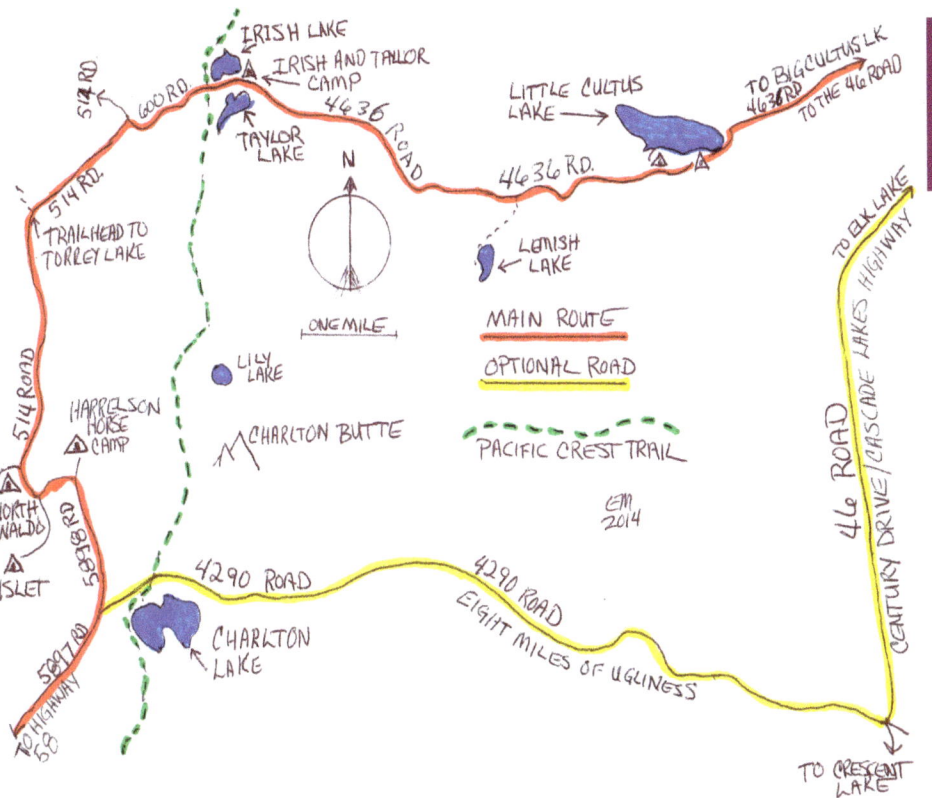

CHARLTON LAKE, PCT & OPTIONAL 4290 ROAD TO THE CASCADE LAKES HIGHWAY

Charlton Lake is a big body of water and probably covers 150 acres or more. The trail from the 4290 Road to the lake is about a quarter-mile long with a smooth and easy path. It's feasible to drag or roll small boats or canoes to water's edge to access more remote parts of the lake. Motors are not allowed.

Fishing for brook trout can be good early in the season and then again in the fall. Fly fishermen do best here in early fall. The PCT edges along the western side of the lake and the several campsites along the shoreline are frequently used by trail hikers for overnight stays or campers who walk the short way from the road.

Looking south, Gerdine Butte, elevation 6,591 feet, is visible to the left above Charlton Lake. The Twins, elevation 7,362 feet, are visible through the trees to the right.

Northern Oregon Backroads Guide to the PCT

IRISH & TAYLOR ROAD / 514 ROAD: Elevation 5,481 ft.

The next part of our route takes us from Waldo Lake to Irish and Taylor Lakes.

⇨ **Not suitable for passenger cars! Best for four-wheel drive vehicles.**

Up front, I'm going to tell you not to ignore the above warning: this road is rugged. Do you need four-wheel drive? In dry weather, probably not, but **you do need clearance**.

Irish and Taylor Lakes are usually referred to together because they are practically joined at the geographical hip. The road bisects the two lakes with Irish on the north side and Taylor to the south, separated by perhaps as little as 150 yards at their nearest points.

With some ruts and rocks along the way, four-wheel drive means you don't have to beat the equipment (as much). A full-size, two-wheel-drive pickup or van will make it if you don't mind taking a thumping. Smaller all-wheel drive vehicles (imagine a Subaru Outback with bumper stickers) with a short wheelbase and reasonable clearance can make it with some probably tense moments. Mid-size and larger SUVs and pickups with four-wheel drive are the best beasts to navigate this road. I drove my 1969 VW Bug across this road in 1988, and it's about the same today (2020) as it was then (the road, not the Bug), which is to say, crappy.

Since that ancient day in 1988, a fire got loose in this lake-studded area north of Waldo Lake and the west side of the Cascade Crest. Shortly after leaving Waldo Lake the road enters the 1996 Charlton Butte fire. While not beautiful by standards of the average human eye, it's interesting to see nature's power to reclaim this once blazing inferno. After crossing the crest into the Deschutes National Forest, the road enters green forest. The **Taylor Burn Road** that heads west from the 600 Road intersection (contrary to its name) also enters green forest.

Don't try this road unless you like challenging conditions and driving at not much more than a walking pace. The total mileage is only about 14 miles with the last 3 miles an improved (10-minute drive) gravel road. Doesn't sound too bad, right?

Estimating that the average human can travel on foot (at a fast walking pace) about 3 miles an hour…it'll take about 3 hours (more time if you stop along the way) to hit pavement. Count on this road

Region 5 — Willamette Pass to Elk Lake

being snowed-in typically until early summer at best. Be prepared to fend for yourself if you break down or get stuck in a snowdrift. Oh yeah, did I mention the skeeters? The many lakes dotting this area also breed many mosquitoes through July and into August.

So what's the pay-off you ask? The rough roads are of course limiting to many travelers so not much traffic (you'll see no Winnebagos). Beautiful, quiet, secluded lakes await paddlers and fishermen at **Irish and Taylor Lakes**. There are many adventure opportunities in the Irish and Taylor Lakes area for hikers and explorers. A mile east of Irish and Taylor Lakes, the **Many Lakes Trailhead** beckons hikers to the nearby **Hanks Lakes** and more fishing, swimming, and camping possibilities in the myriad lakes scattered about this basin.

Still want to go? I salute you my brave (or foolish) friend…this book is subtitled *Northern Oregon Backroads Guide* and roads in Oregon don't get much more "backroad" than this one… Let the games begin.

The 514 Road starts out from the entrance to North Waldo Campground and heads north. A couple of potential campsites in the forest present themselves as we leave North Waldo. The road starts out rough and nasty and pretty much stays that way for many miles to Little Cultus Lake.

Charlton Lake is an easy walk from the road. Gerdine Butte is in the background.

In less than a half-mile, we enter the massive **Charlton Fire** of 1996 (more than 10,000 acres consumed). The burned forest is a stark reminder of nature's forces. With thin soils and short growing seasons, new life is slowly healing the landscape. Young trees (and wildflowers in the early summer) are now well established and the charred woods against a background of blue skies can be strangely beautiful.

Plenty of little twists in the road lie ahead, but we drive almost due north for 2 miles before the road bends northeast. It's at this point we find a parking area next to the road and the trailhead to large (about 70 acres) Torrey Lake.

Torrey Lake Trailhead: There's not much room to park at the trailhead but luckily, traffic is rare. Squeeze in where you can without blocking the road. No signs mark the trail but it's plainly visible from this corner, heading uphill and west.

After about a mile the trail forks to the right for Torrey Lake. Head straight ahead from the fork for nearby **Wahanna Lake**. The big fire consumed the forest right to the edge of Torrey and Wahanna Lakes.

Volunteer fish stockers occasionally stock Wahanna and Torrey with juvenile rainbow trout. As plants and insect communities continue to re-establish themselves around the lake edges, early in the year is the time to target those fisheries.

As the road leaves the Torrey Lake Trailhead, it continues rocky and rough but finds a way through or around every obstacle. We'll bounce our way northeast another 1.5 miles to the junction with the #600 Road.

INTERSECTION 514 & 600 ROADS: Elevation 5,527 ft.

The rocky road to the right (east) is the Main Route and continues uphill to the crest of the Cascades where we enter Deschutes County and leave the burned forest behind. It's at this point **the 600 Road becomes the 4636 Road** as we enter the Deschutes National Forest, cross the Pacific Crest Trail, and arrive at **Irish and Taylor Lakes**.

The **road to the left at this intersection (heading west)** is the continuation of the #514 Road and heads towards the **Taylor Burn** area. The Taylor Burn Road is extremely rough but it goes through (mostly) unburned forest. It's just like the rough, gnarly roads you've driven already to get to this point and four-wheel drive is recommended.

Region 5 — Willamette Pass to Elk Lake

Checking the map at beautiful Taylor Lake.

More lakes are accessible by easy hikes from the Taylor Burn Road. Near the end of the road is the Taylor Burn Guard station, elevation 5,226 feet, with a picnic table and fire-ring outside. An ancient car-camp is adjacent, complete with an ancient outhouse. Trailheads leading to the popular **Erma Bell Lakes** northwest of here are rarely used from this side. Nearby **Edna Lake** is good sized and accessed by trail from here. There are some other lakes in the area with one nice easy trail from near the Guard Station to a small lake to the southeast.

IRISH AND TAYLOR LAKES: Elevation: 5,565 ft.

After crossing the Cascade Crest and entering the **Deschutes National Forest**, the 600 Road becomes the 4636 Road. The road bisects the two lakes with Irish Lake on the north and slightly bigger Taylor Lake to the south. A large, heavily used campground is adjacent to Irish Lake. There are no facilities at either lake. Small boats can be slipped into either lake; no motors are allowed.

The fishing is usually more productive at Irish Lake so it gets the most use, while Taylor Lake is on the quieter side of the road. **The PCT passes each lake on the west side.** Despite their remoteness, the several hike-in lakes in the Irish and Taylor area are popular with fishermen and hikers. Taylor Lake is great for the paddler with inlets

Northern Oregon Backroads Guide to the PCT

A good place to fish at East Hanks Lake.

and interesting coves for exploring. Irish Lake is really two lakes joined by a shallow channel.

Like all of the lakes in this region of the High Cascades, fishing is best shortly after ice-off. This means that snowmobilers have the best shot at good fishing because the roads are clogged with snow until the end of June in most years.

Typically, by the end of October the weather can get dicey at these elevations. On the bright side, the skeeters are done by late August and days can be sunny and warm during late summer. Mid-September is the time to be hiking, camping, fishing, and exploring these environs.

ROAD 4636: IRISH & TAYLOR LAKES TO CASCADE LAKES HIGHWAY

⇨ **Not recommended for passenger cars!**

The good news is that the pavement is only 8 miles away and the last 3 miles of the 4636 Road is improved gravel. The bad news is the 4636 Road between Irish and Taylor and Little Cultus Lakes is a 4-mile-per-hour road at best. Figure about an hour to Little Cultus with a fifteen-minute stop to calm your jangled nerves along the way. After leaving Irish and Taylor Lakes the road heads east and

Region 5 — Willamette Pass to Elk Lake

downhill over rocks and ruts for about 1.5 miles before coming to the Many Lakes Trailhead parking area on our left.

Many Lakes Trailhead: Elevation: 5,368 feet

As the name implies, this trail heads north into the **Three Sisters Wilderness**, passing near many lakes. Three good-size lakes near the trailhead are collectively called the Hanks Lakes with **East Hanks Lake** the first encountered to the right in less then a quarter-mile. Next is **Middle Hanks Lake** with the trail splitting to the left to the largest of the three, **West Hanks Lake**. Each of the three lakes holds brook trout and/or rainbows. The main trail heads north past many more lakes before heading east past (guess what?) more lakes ending eventually at Cultus Lake. Several more lakes to the east off the main trail have boot beaten paths to them for the route-finding fishermen among us.

LITTLE CULTUS LAKE AREA

"Little" is a bit of a misnomer in this case; Little Cultus is a good-size lake and easily covers more than 160 acres. More fisherman-friendly than "Big" Cultus Lake, the lake is a popular fishery with brook trout and rainbows available. Motors are allowed but there's a 10 mph speed limit on the lake.

Cultus Lake Resort has beautifully landscaped grounds.

Little Cultus Lake Campground: Elevation 4,774 ft.

Little Cultus Lake Campground is laid out on the southeast side of the lake. The boat launch and day use area divide the two lobes of the campground. Facilities include accessible vault toilets and water. There are also a couple of unimproved drive-in sites on the northeast side of Little Cultus Lake. Just past the campground, we meet a road to our left that edges along the north side of the lake. This side road continues to good-sized **Deer Lake** and a trail to **West Cultus Lake Campground**. A spur road heads up to Cultus Mountain (elevation 5,759 ft.).

From the Little Cultus Campground, the 4636 Road continues northeast past Little Cultus Lake. The 4636 Road is washboarded in places but otherwise its about 2.5 miles and clear sailing to the stop sign and the intersection with the **Cultus Lake / 4635 Road**.

INTERSECTION 4636 & 4635 ROADS: Elevation 4,535 ft.

The Main Route turns right (east) and follows the 4635 Road to the Cascade Lakes Highway (See description below). Turn left (west) and the 4635 Road takes you to (Big) Cultus Lake Campground and Cultus Lake Resort.

CULTUS LAKE AREA: Elevation 4,676 feet at the surface.

Cultus (the word means "useless" in Chinook jargon) is one of the largest natural lakes in the region and sits in a glacier-scooped basin. The big lake is over 200 feet deep with a surface area of around 1,140 acres. Beware! If you're seeking peace and quiet, Cultus is one of the few lakes in the area with no speed limit, attracting jet-skis and water skiers during the summer months.

Besides the drive-in Cultus Lake Campground, several informal boat-in (or hike-in) campsites are along the north shore of the lake. A developed site is at **Big Cove**. On the extreme western end of the lake is the **West Cultus Campground**, also most conveniently accessed by boat.

Early in the season is the time to target the lake's big (12–15 lb.) lake trout, with ice-off finding the mackinaw hungry and close to shore. As the water warms, the macks head toward deeper holes where they tease the fishermen on the fishfinder but refuse to bite. Rainbow trout fishing is mostly done on the troll with the area north and west from the resort sometimes productive. Water depths drop off quickly, so stick close to shore when targeting 'bows.

Region 5 — Willamette Pass to Elk Lake

Cultus Lake Campground: Located on the eastern end of the lake, the campground has a boat launch and 60 fee sites. The campground and day-use area are extremely popular during summer weekends, and the boat launch can be a zoo. The day-use area is pleasant with a swim area and great western exposure during summer afternoons. Look for a campsite farthest from the boat launch for some semblance of peace and quiet. The **Winopee Trailhead** is located at Cultus Lake Campground and heads west along Cultus Lake's north shore, connecting with the Big Cove and West Cultus Campgrounds.

Cultus Lake Resort
541-480-7378

Situated on the southeast side of the lake and separated from the campground by Cultus Creek, the resort has 23 cabins, a restaurant, store, and marina. Besides power boats they also rent canoes, kayaks, and paddleboards. The resort prides itself on its extensive flower gardens and beautiful lawn. Custom rock steps lead from the lawn to the beach and swimming area.

The restaurant serves breakfast, lunch, and dinner during the summer season and also caters weddings and other small events at the resort. The store is well stocked and sells fishing tackle. Fish stories and fishing advice are free.

Quieter times prevail in the early fall at Cultus Lake.

Northern Oregon Backroads Guide to the PCT

CASCADE LAKES HIGHWAY / CULTUS LAKE ROAD INTERSECTION: Elevation 4,480 ft.

As we meet up with the Cascade Lakes Highway, we are presented with two options. Unseen, but directly ahead of us is Crane Prairie Reservoir. The Main Route heads north (left) to Elk Lake if you want to skip exploring the Crane Prairie area.

Crane Prairie Reservoir Area: Turn right (south) from the Cultus Lake Road and drive about 2.4 miles to the turn-off to **Quinn River Campground** (41 sites and a boat launch) and the trailhead to **Osprey Point**, both situated on the west side of Crane Prairie Reservoir. The crystal clear **Quinn River** flows from a large spring adjacent to the campground and heads east a short way to the reservoir. The trail to Osprey Point begins at the parking area just north of the big springs. There are actually several springs in the immediate area, part of the extensive underground plumbing in this porous volcanic landscape.

Another 1.5 miles south of Quinn River along the 46 Road is the **Rock Creek Campground** and boat launch (31 fee sites) with beautiful views across the water to Mt. Bachelor.

The view from Crane Prairie Resort features (from l to r) South Sister, Broken Top, and Mount Bachelor.

Region 5 — Willamette Pass to Elk Lake

MAP R5.4: CRANE PRAIRIE RESERVOIR

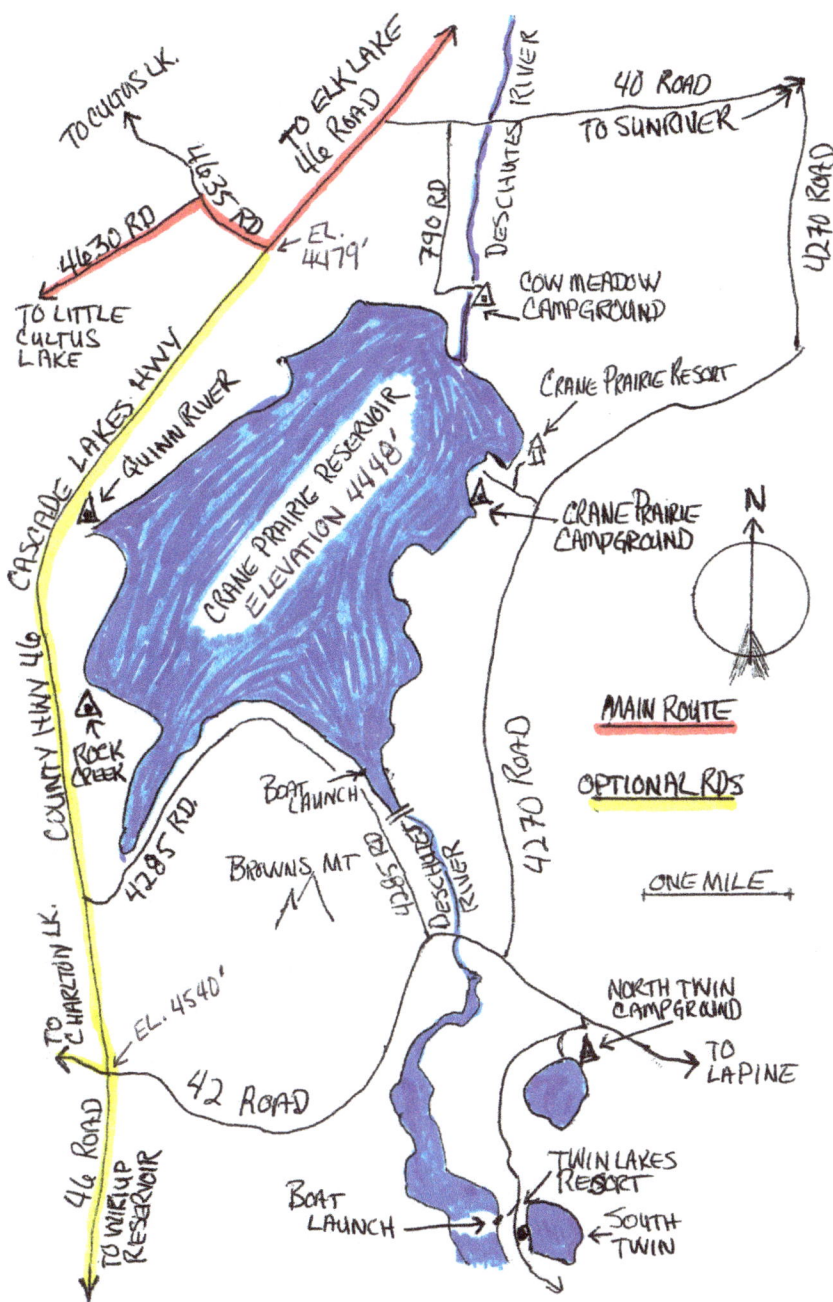

The reservoir covers over 5 square miles and is formed by a dam on the Deschutes River. **Crane Prairie Resort** and **Crane Prairie Campground** (140 sites and a boat launch) are located on the northeast side of the lake close to where the river runs in. **Cow Meadow Campground** is located directly on the Deschutes, just upstream from its confluence with the reservoir and is the best choice for campers seeking quiet. There's a boat launch of sorts at the campground best suited for canoes and kayaks.

Many, many informal campsites surround Crane Prairie if you want to look for them on the south and east sides of the lake. Some boat campers launch at one of the developed campgrounds and camp along the peaceful (and inaccessible by road) sites along the lake. Early in the season is the best time to be here when the lake is full and the fishing is better.

CASCADE LAKES HIGHWAY

This highway to heaven takes the traveler through some of the most stunning mountain landscapes in Oregon. The dramatic mix of snow-capped volcanoes and the primal feel of the many lakes and streams of this volcanic highland attracts recreation seekers of all stripes.

When the highway was originally completed, it formed a loop of about 100 miles and was popularly referred to as **"The Century Drive."** Road improvements and rerouting have now reduced the total mileage (closer to 86 miles) but signs and locals still refer to the original name.

Today the trend is toward referring to the original Forest Service 46 Road section as "The Cascade Lakes Highway" while the eastern sections closer to and including parts of Highway 97 are still signed "Century Drive." Deschutes County does the bulk of highway maintenance today and calls the shots when closing the highway for the winter.

Those of you who took the Optional Road from Highway 58 to reach the Cultus Lake Road have taken a peek at the beauty of the Cascade Lakes Highway passing by **Davis Lake, Wickiup Reservoir,** and **Crane Prairie Reservoir**. As the snow melts off in late spring and early summer, it's not unusual on sunny days to find throngs of hikers mixing with campers, fly fishermen, sailors, and snowmobilers. Paddling sports of all kinds are popular on the many lakes and streams found in the Cascade Lakes area west of the city of Bend. After the snow flies, snow sport lovers find downhill skiing

Region 5 — Willamette Pass to Elk Lake

opportunities at **Mount Bachelor** and the network of cross-country ski trails in the surrounding area.

Cultus Lake Road to Elk Lake Resort: Elk Lake Resort is a good source for information about local snow conditions and winter road closures of the Cascade Lakes Highway.

Elk Lake Resort
541-480-7378 • elklakeresort.net

The Cascades Lakes Highway is not plowed in the winter between Mount Bachelor Ski Area and Elk Lake Resort, and when the snows begin in earnest, the Cascade Lakes Highway is gated closer to Crane Prairie Reservoir, well south of Elk Lake. At any rate, **Elk Lake Resort is not accessible by cars or four-wheel drive in the winter**. Guests can cross country ski or snowmobile to the lodge and the resort offers **snow-cat service** on a regular schedule, departing from near the Mount Bachelor Ski Area, that coordinates with public transportation from Bend.

LAVA LAKES AREA

As we head north on the Cascade Lakes Highway, we soon come to the turn-off to Lava Lakes on our right. It's a short drive to the fork in

Big Lava Lake awaits the early morning paddler.

Northern Oregon Backroads Guide to the PCT

Snow-covered Mount Bachelor looms above Little Lava Lake.

the road; Lava Lake Resort and the Lava Lake Campground are to the left, and Little Lava Lake is to the right.

"Big" Lava Lake is a beautiful place indeed with views across the lake of Mount Bachelor, Broken Top, and South Sister. The 370-acre lake is spring fed and supports a healthy food chain that grows healthy fish. Fishermen target the lake early in the year for rainbow and brook trout. Rainbows over 20 inches are regularly caught here with many fish in the 15-inch range boated. Still-fishing with power bait is popular off the northeastern point called "Velveeta Point." Trollers catch fish using small lures and spinners spiked with a tiny piece of worm. There's a 10 mph limit on Lava.

Lava Lake Campground: This campground has 22 fee sites and a boat launch. The campground is popular and usually packed on summer weekends. A trail along the east side of Lava Lake heads north from the camp and a side path leads down to Velveeta Point and a place to fish from the bank.

Lava Lake Resort
541-383-9443

The resort is located at the south end of the lake and has a large RV park with full hookups. The resort rents motor boats and paddle

Region 5 — Willamette Pass to Elk Lake

MAP R5.5: CASCADE LAKES HIGHWAY

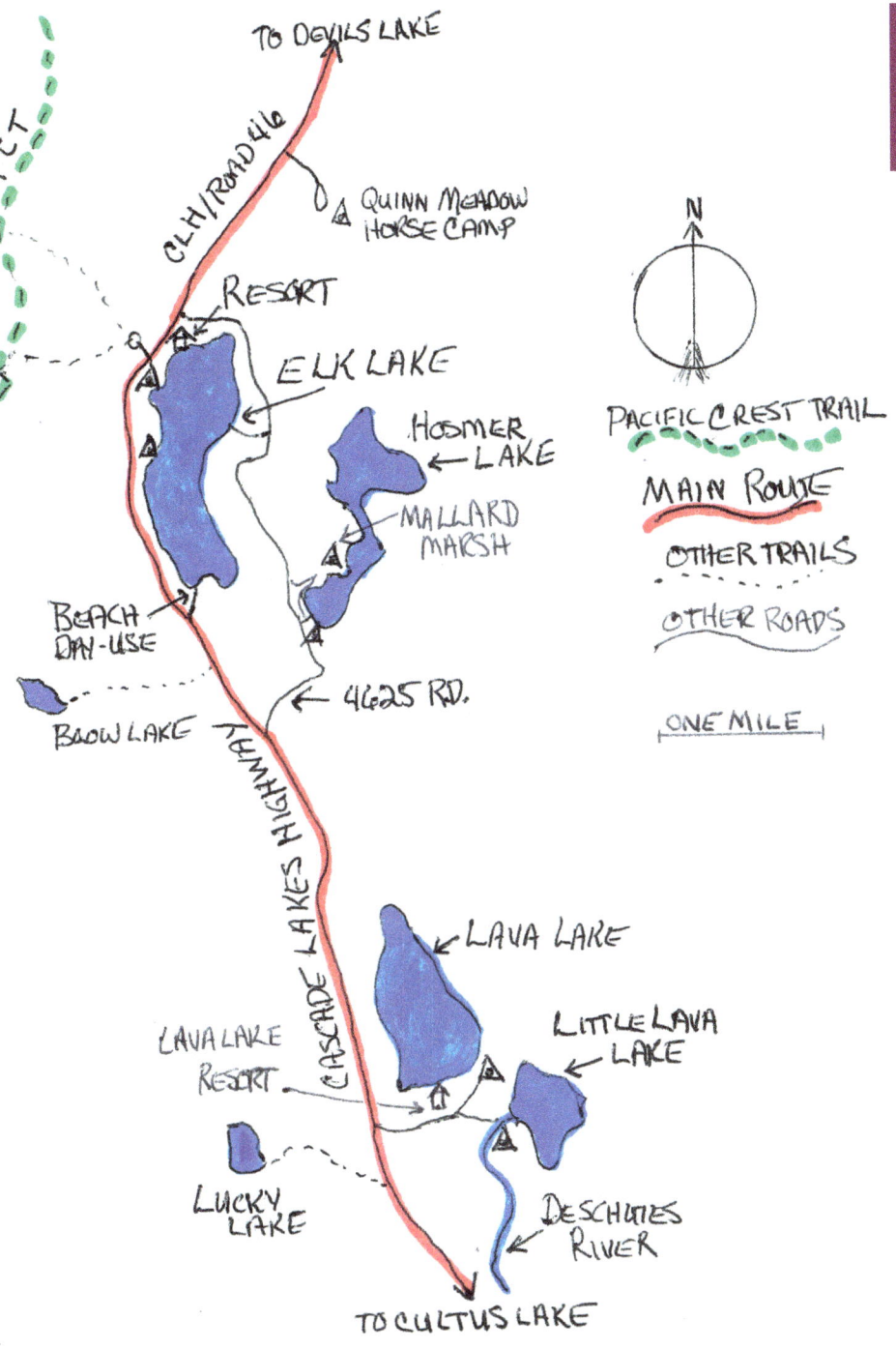

Northern Oregon Backroads Guide to the PCT

Hosmer Lake has a primal "dawn of time" feel.

craft, including canoes and kayaks. The small store has basic items for campers and fishermen but no café or bar. Showers and laundry facilities are adjacent to the RV park. There's also a small marina with gas for boats.

Little Lava Lake is less then a half-mile from the road fork and has a pleasant campground with a boat launch. This spring-fed lake covers about 120 surface acres and is recognized as the **source of the mighty Deschutes River**. The beautiful surroundings, nearby volcanoes, and abundant wildlife lend a primal feel to this lake. Fishing on Little Lava is generally less productive then nearby Lava Lake so it's usually quieter than Big Lava. No motors are allowed on Little Lava.

Little Lava Campground is located on the west side of the lake and has 10 fee sites along with a boat launch. A trail heads north from Little Lava and takes the hiker to Lava Lake Campground.

As we leave Lava Lakes and head north on Highway 46, our next major road to the right is the road to Hosmer Lake and the Elk Lake Loop Road (the Loop Road is described in Region Six).

Hosmer Lake: Hosmer Lake, like Little Lava Lake, has a timeless feel. With bulrushes along the shore and the freshly made feel of

Region 5 — Willamette Pass to Elk Lake

the lava strewn landscape, it wouldn't be surprising (almost) to see a wooly mammoth grazing in the shallows early on a misty morning. Wildlife of the more modern era is abundant in these surroundings. Water birds of all kinds frequent these environs in different seasons.

The lake is managed as a quality fishery with barbless fly fishing only. Electric motors are allowed on the lake. There's a small campground here with a nearby boat launch. Rainbow and brook trout are found here along with **Atlantic salmon**.

The fishing can be a beautiful but frustrating experience. The water is crystal clear and the fish are plainly visible, which means of course that you appear crystal clear to the fish. It's so beautiful here with the big volcanoes staring at you that you might not even care that the fish are taunting you. The serene environment makes for a great paddling experience even when the fish won't bite.

Two campgrounds are at Hosmer: South Campground with 23 sites is adjacent to the boat launch. **Mallard Marsh Campground** is towards the north and features a short and level path to a slide-in **boat launch for small craft**. Look for the path to the boat launch between campsites 14 and 15. The launch has a tiny dock and a canoe rack.

Back on the Cascade Lakes Highway we quickly come to Elk Lake, Beach Day-Use Area, and the beginning of Region Six.

REGION FIVE WRAP-UP

In Region Five we've started out in western Oregon at Willamette Pass, then traveled across the Cascade Crest to the stunning Cascade Lakes Area west of the city of Bend. The Cascade Lakes are a year-round playground with some of the best opportunities in Oregon for hiking, fishing, camping, and snow sports.

In Region Six, we'll continue our exploration of the high lakes before traveling north along the rough but very beautiful 370 Road to the Three Creek Lake area, the town of Sisters, and the end of Region Six at Santiam Pass.

MAP R6.1: ELK LAKE TO SANTIAM PASS

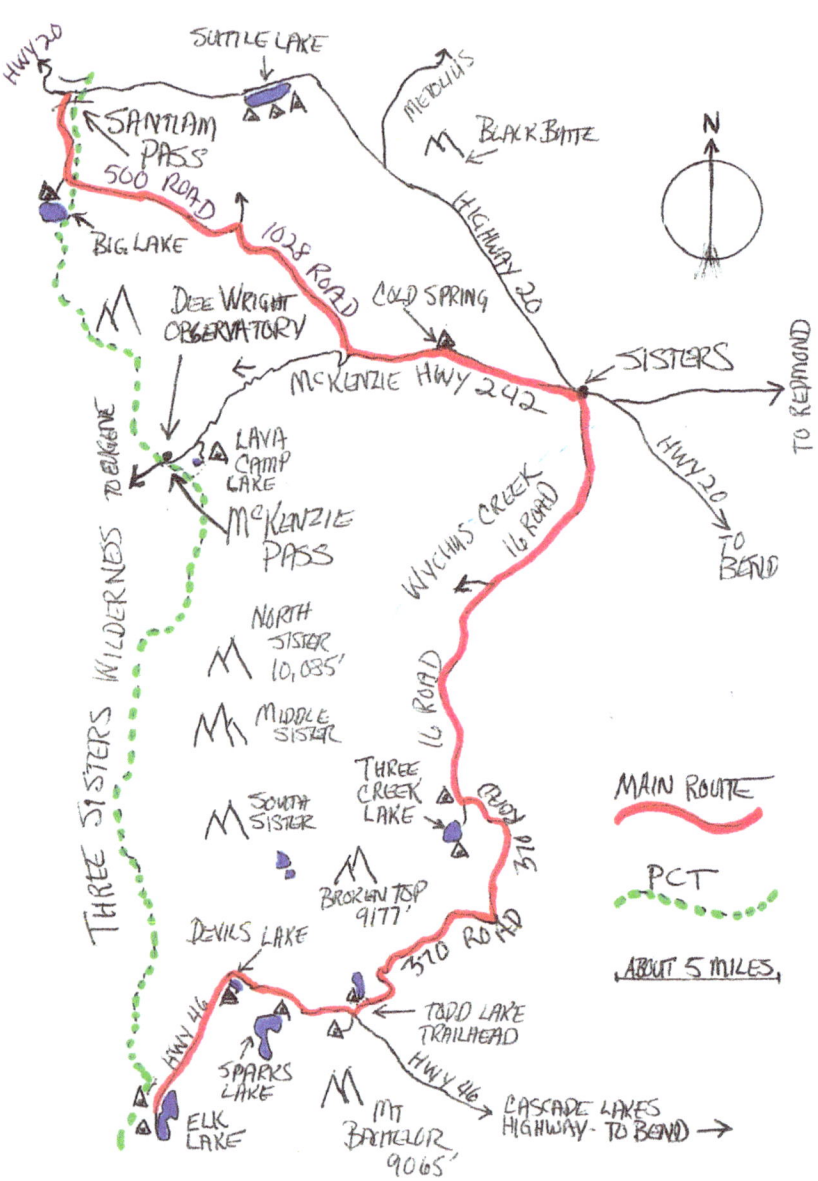

REGION SIX
Elk Lake to Santiam Pass

Sailing at Elk Lake.

"Would you tell me, please,
which way I ought to go from here?"
"That depends a good deal on where you
want to get to," said the Cat.

— *Lewis Carroll,* **Alice in Wonderland**

Region 6 — Elk Lake to Santiam Pass

ROUTE DESCRIPTION

The Main Route continues north along the Cascade Lakes Highway from Elk Lake. On the way to our turn-off at Todd Lake, we'll explore the walk-in campground at Devils Lake, the drive-in campground at Soda Creek, and the day-use area at Sparks Lake.

> ⇨ **The 370 Road past the Todd Lake Trailhead is rough (not suitable for passenger cars) but crosses some stunning parkland with many hiking opportunities at the foot of Broken Top Mountain.**
>
> ⇨ **Allow at least 8 hours to drive this entire route.**

We'll wind through woodland and meadow before fording the North Fork of Tumalo Creek. The 370 Road ends at Forest Road 16 near Three Creek Lake. After exploring the Tam McArthur Rim – Three Creek Lake area, we'll head downhill on the paved Forest Road 16 to the town of Sisters.

Following a brief exploration of Sisters, we'll hook up with the paved McKenzie Pass Highway 242 (the optional side trip to McKenzie Pass and the Dee Wright Observatory are described below). After passing the Cold Spring riparian area and campground, we'll turn north onto gravel Forest Road 1028, traveling northwest to our intersection with the more primitive 500 Road (not recommended for passenger vehicles).

We'll head due west on the old Santiam Wagon Road – 500 Road, crossing the Pacific Crest Trail before encountering Big Lake. From Big Lake the paved 2690 Road heads past the Hoodoo Ski Bowl before delivering us to Santiam Pass and the end of Region Six.

I've been kicking around this region for a lot of years and feel I've just scratched the surface. Take a few days (or years) to really explore this part of Oregon's High Cascades. With tasty restaurants, trendy breweries, and year-round recreational opportunities nearby, the city of Bend is well worth your time. The town of Sisters attracts many visitors to town by hosting a variety of events throughout the year. The scenic beauty of the area speaks for itself.

ROAD CONDITIONS

Other than the two roads described below, all of the roads in Region Six are passable by regular passenger vehicles during favorable weather conditions.

> ⇦ *Stark lava fields and North Sister dominate the southern horizon from McKenzie Pass.*

- The 370 Road connecting Todd Lake (near Mt. Bachelor) to Three Creek Lake is best suited to four-wheel-drive, high-clearance vehicles.
- The other road to avoid if you're driving a low-clearance vehicle is the 500 Road – Old Santiam Wagon Road west of Sisters and near Santiam Pass.

RECOMMENDED MAPS FOR REGION SIX

The Deschutes National Forest map is available at the Ranger Station in Sisters or the National Forest Headquarters in Bend, 541-383-5300. For information and to order maps on-line go to fs.fed.us/r6/Deschutes. The *Oregon Road and Recreation Atlas*, published by Benchmark Maps is available at outdoor and recreation stores or benchmarkmaps.com.

- Deschutes National Forest visitors map.
- Page 62 of the *Oregon Road and Recreation Atlas*.

OPTIONAL ROUTES & ROADS IN REGION SIX

If you have a high-clearance vehicle, preferably four-wheel-drive, you can explore some of the less accessible areas in Region Six. If not, follow the optional routes below.

Optional Route One: The Todd Lake – 370 Road to Three Creek Lake should only be attempted by high-clearance vehicles. Consult map R6.3. From the Todd Lake intersection, follow Highway 46 east to the City of Bend to avoid the 370 Road.

Navigating the City of Bend. Our goal is to head north on Highway 97 from Bend. But beware of the learning curve when it comes to navigating through Bend. Even I (Mr. Map Guy, as my friends call me) get off-course nearly every time when approaching town from the Cascade Lakes Highway.

The street intersections in many parts of Bend are laid-out in roundabouts. Roundabouts are great once you get used to them. Locals seem to be in a hurry to get wherever they're going and frown upon vehicular indecision. So, if you're uninitiated to the rules of the roundabout, pretend like you know what you're doing and keep circling to the left… The city surely has a "Thou shalt circle Left but only turn Right" czar who dreams nightly about constantly flowing traffic.

Region 6 — Elk Lake to Santiam Pass

Try to pay attention to the signs directing you to Highway 97 as you circle about and don't be afraid to go around twice (or thrice) if you have doubts. Colorado Avenue is the most direct route so keep an eye out for that street as the steering wheel spins around.

After we cross the Deschutes River, Colorado Avenue is the street to follow southeast to meet up with Highway 97 North. After merging with Highway 97, we head north towards Redmond. Take the marked exit to the town of Sisters and Highway 20 west. Head several miles west on Highway 20 to Sisters where we'll rejoin the Main Route.

Optional Route Two: The other road to avoid for low-clearance vehicles is the 500 Road – Santiam Wagon Road. Consult Map R6.4.

The old wagon road is not suitable for passenger vehicles. The traveler cursed with a low-clearance vehicle has two options to driving this road.

1. From the town of Sisters, drive west on Highway 20 to Santiam Pass and the end of Region Six.

2. The 1028 Road is part of the Main Route (marked in red on Map R6.4) and heads north from the McKenzie Pass Highway. The 1028 Road is an improved gravel road to its intersection with the rough 500 Road. The 500 Road is the old Santiam Pass Wagon Road and leads west.

At the 500/1028 Roads intersection, the road to the right and leading northeast is the 2067 Road. If you have a map and plenty of gas, this road is improved and delivers you to Santiam Pass – Highway 20 near Suttle Lake. Head west on Highway 20 to Santiam Pass and the end of Region Six.

Optional McKenzie Pass Hwy. to Dee Wright Observatory:
McKenzie Pass – Highway 242 begins at the town of Sisters. This optional route describes the highway past the intersection of the 1028 Road, taking the traveler west to another access point on the Pacific Crest Trail and an exploration of Dee Wright Observatory.

Northern Oregon Backroads Guide to the PCT

⇨ **Warning:** *The high elevation portion of the McKenzie Pass Highway is closed to vehicles or combinations exceeding 35 feet at all times. The upper highway is not plowed and is gated from November to July in most years.*

Windy Point. If the weather is clear, it's one of those places that will make you go "wow" every time. Windy Point is the first spot along the westbound McKenzie Pass Highway to stop and see a small part of the vast lava fields covering this part of the high Cascades. Interpretive signs point out local landmarks and offer a brief explanation of what lies before our eyes.

Keep in mind as we drive further southwest and uphill from Windy Point, the modern highway is built on the course of the old McKenzie Pass Wagon Road. The builders cut a rough and rocky way through the lava fields covering the summit area. The road is very narrow and in places, the sheer lava walls rise from the narrow shoulder.

At first glance the lava fields appear barren of life but nature is slowly reclaiming the land. Interspersed among the lava fields we see what are referred to as "tree islands", places where the lava flowed around high point barriers providing habitat for plants and animals.

Looking north from Windy Point, lava fields stretch nearly to the horizon. Mount Washington is in the distance.

Region 6 — Elk Lake to Santiam Pass

A direction finder atop Dee Wright Observatory points out local volcanoes.

PCT/Lava Camp Lake Campground. The road is a bit rough but OK for any vehicle. After heading uphill we come to a fork with the road to the right leading to a trailhead access with a large parking lot and turn-around. There are a few campsites near the parking area with picnic tables and fire-rings. The trail intersects the PCT a very short way past the parking lot, and then heads south to North Matthieu Lake and Scott Pass. The northbound **Pacific Crest Trail** heads sharply west from this intersection as hikers traverse the lava fields parallel to the highway before crossing the road west of the Dee Wright Observatory.

From the road fork, the road to the left takes us to Lava Camp Lake Campground with ten campsites. The lake is tiny but the clear waters are great for swimming on a hot summer day. There are vault toilets but no drinking water. This is a good place to headquarter in late summer for day hike explorations into the surrounding high country. Another tiny lake lies just east of Lava Camp Lake; follow the footpath a few hundred yards to Little Lava Camp Lake.

Dee Wright Observatory - McKenzie Pass Summit. Looking like it morphed from the surrounding lava fields, the roundhouse structure of Dee Wright Observatory dominates the summit of

Northern Oregon Backroads Guide to the PCT

McKenzie Pass. Not an astronomical observatory, Dee Wright is perched above the highway to show the locations of the surrounding mountain peaks through slots in the building's walls.

Park below and walk the winding path to the observatory on a clear day and you'll see more lava lying around than you thought possible. On the tip-top of the structure there's a 360-degree view of this Vulcan wonderland along with a pointer to surrounding points of geological interest. A half-mile-long trail with interpretive signs connects to the observatory and allows the stroller (OK for wheelchairs too) to get a better sense of the dynamics of the lava flows seen here and more views of the surrounding volcanoes.

The Dee Wright Observatory structure was completed in 1935 by the Civilian Conservation Corps and was named after a long-time Forest Service employee who died in 1934 after serving 24 years as a Forest Service packer and foreman at Camp Belknap. Just west of the observatory is the trailhead parking area for the **Pacific Crest Trail**.

From the summit of McKenzie Pass, Highway 242 heads west to the town of McKenzie Bridge. This is not a high-speed highway and has many sharp curves as you wind your way down. If you choose to explore much further west along this road, plan extra time.

PCT ACCESS POINTS

Four access points to the PCT are in Region Six, Map R6.1

1. Region Six begins at Elk Lake and a short trail connection to the Pacific Crest Trail.
2. The next road connection to the PCT is at McKenzie Pass. It is 31 trail miles from Elk Lake.
3. The next access point to the PCT is near Big Lake along the 500 Road.
4. Region Six ends at Santiam Pass. The PCT parking area is accessed by a short road. From McKenzie Pass, it is 17.5 trail miles to reach Santiam Pass.

Dee Wright was a packer for the Forest Sevice. This photo shows him near Sahalie Falls with his horse and dog.

Northern Oregon Backroads Guide to the PCT

MAIN ROADS IN ORDER OF TRAVEL

All road descriptions are south to north.

Cascade Lakes Highway – Road 46	This paved road takes us north from Elk Lake (gas is available at Elk Lake Resort) to the Todd Lake – 370 Road intersection.
Todd Lake Road – 370 Road	After leaving the Todd Lake Trailhead, this unimproved dirt road (not recommended for passenger cars) heads north past Broken Top Trailhead to an intersection with Forest Road 16 near Three Creek Lake.
Forest Road 16	This gravel road becomes paved about a mile downhill from the 370 Road Intersection; it's about 15 miles downhill (north) to the town of Sisters and the McKenzie Pass Highway.
Highway 20	We are on this State Highway for a few city blocks through the town of Sisters. The turn-off to the McKenzie Pass Highway is on the western edge of town.
McKenzie Pass – Highway 242	The paved highway heads west from Sisters, past the Cold Spring Campground to the intersection with Forest Road 1028.
Forest Road 1028	The 1028 Road heads north from the McKenzie Pass Highway and is the improved gravel road connection to Forest Road 500
Forest Road 500	This rough, dirt road (not recommended for passenger cars) is the old Santiam Pass wagon road. After meeting up with the PCT near Big Lake, the 500 Road ends at the intersection with Forest Road 2690.
Forest Road 2690	This paved road connects the Forest Service campgrounds at Big Lake with Highway 20 and Santiam Pass. Santiam Pass is the end of Region Six.

Region 6 — Elk Lake to Santiam Pass

MAP R6.2: ELK LAKE TO TODD LAKE TRAILHEAD

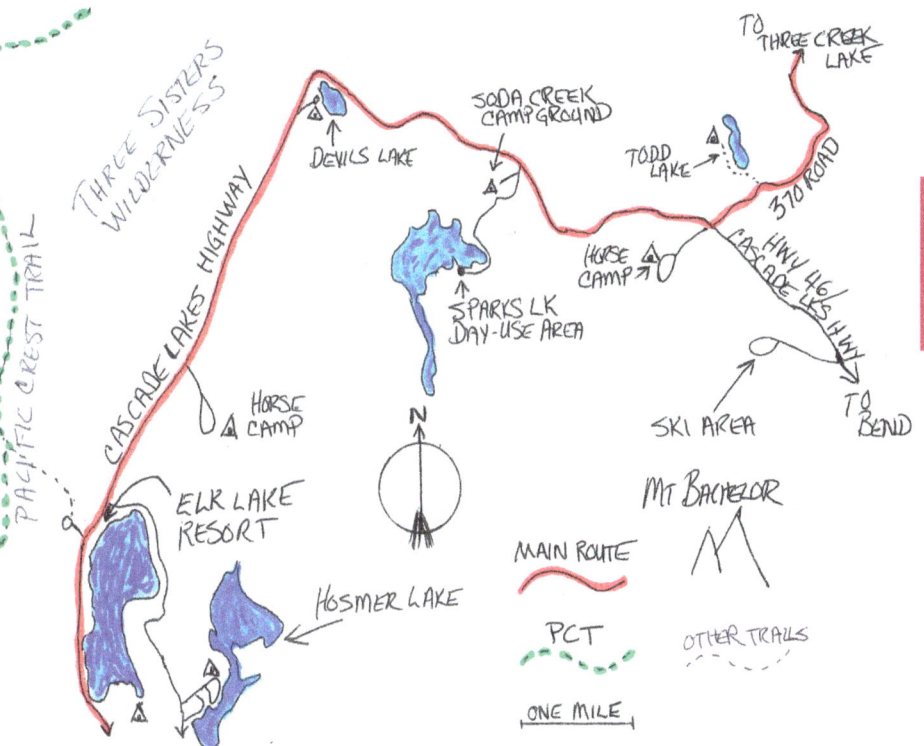

ROAD NOTES – REGION SIX

Starting at Elk Lake and Elk Lake Resort, we will be heading first to the Todd Lake Trailhead. The following notes describe the sights and attractions along our route.

ELK LAKE: Elevation 4,889 feet at the surface.

Elk Lake is a popular recreation lake spanning over 400 acres and can be packed with sun seekers on summer days. In the winter, the Cascade Lakes Highway from Bend is not plowed and is gated at the Mt Bachelor Ski Area. To the south of Elk Lake, the Cascade Lakes Highway is usually gated near Forest Highway 40 after the snow flies.

Snow sports ranging from snowshoeing to snowmobiling are available, and the usually abundant powder makes snow lovers flock to this winter wonderland. **Elk Lake Resort** is open year-round and also rents cabins to those who just want to enjoy the many days of sunny winter weather.

Northern Oregon Backroads Guide to the PCT

A late spring day at Beach Day-Use Area, Elk Lake.

The summer season is short at these elevations, with Elk Lake and some of the other high elevation lakes sporting snow until late June and well into July in some heavy snow years. When the lake becomes liquid and the summer sun is high, paddlers and sailors outnumber anglers after midday. Kokanee and brook trout are the main target for fishermen. Like most of the high lakes west of Bend, fishing is best shortly after ice-off in May. The mid-fall weather can be beautiful, and fly fishing can be very productive when the fish are eager to stock up for the winter.

Elk Lake Resort: Located on the northwest side of Elk Lake, the resort plays host to water sports lovers of all descriptions. The parking area can look like a used watercraft lot on hot summer weekends. There's a restaurant and bar, and the resort hosts live music on their outdoor beer garden stage during the summer. Perhaps of particular interest to PCT hikers, the resort has ice cream, burgers, and beer.

Hikers from around the world are drawn to the challenge of the Pacific Crest Trail, so it isn't unusual to meet people from all points of the globe at Elk Lake Resort. **A short side trail connects the PCT to the resort** and thru-hikers use the resort as a re-supply point before heading north through the remainder of the Three Sisters Wilderness and the PCT's next road junction near McKenzie Pass.

Region 6 — Elk Lake to Santiam Pass

The Marina at Elk Lake Resort is packed with boats and folks on a warm summer weekend.

The resort rents cabins that range from upscale to rustic with prices ranging between the two. The rustic camper cabins are very basic with propane heat, a picnic table, and a fire ring.

There's a marina with boat fuel available dockside. The marina rents floating craft from paddleboards to power boats. There's a (sometimes crowded) boat launch open to the public for a $5 fee. The **Elk Lake Campground** is right next door and also has a good boat launch.

During the snow months, the resort offers transportation to and from the Mt. Bachelor Ski Area parking lot to Elk Lake Resort using their tracked "Snoburbans." Regular bus service to the Mount Bachelor Ski Area from the town of Bend coordinates with the Resort's scheduled transportation. For current road conditions contact **Elk Lake Resort** at 541-480-7378 or look for links and general information on their website: elklakeresort.net

CAMPGROUNDS & DAY-USE SITES IN THE ELK LAKE AREA

Beach Day-Use Area is located on the southern end of Elk Lake and is popular with families for the gentle, pumice beach. The day-use area is a great spot to observe the **South Sister volcano** and with sail boats on the water, the views can be quite spectacular. Picnic tables along the beach area and vault toilets are the only amenities here.

Sunset View Day-Use Area is on the lake's eastern shore and is popular with the sailing and paddling crowd.

Elk Lake Campground is adjacent to the resort and has a good boat launch. The 21 campsites are situated along the rather steep road leading down to the shoreline and are within easy walking distance to Elk Lake Resort. This campground is extremely popular, and it can be tough to find a campsite in the busy season; midweek is the best time to grab a spot here.

Point Campground is on the lake's southwestern side next to the road. Point has just nine units and fills up quickly during the summer. The campground features a boat launch and is a fully accessible facility.

Little Fawn Group Camp is located on the lake's southeastern shore with 12 sites. The campground requires reservations and accommodates trailers to 30 feet.

Back on Highway 46 Heading North from Elk Lake: The first road we encounter on our right as we leave Elk Lake Resort is the 4625 Road, the loop road around Elk Lake. Near the intersection there's a restored Forest Guard Station that is worth checking out if you're a history buff. Past the Guard Station the 4625 Road turns to gravel and heads south following the east side of Elk Lake. The road can be washboarded and heads downhill before passing the Sunset View Day-Use Area and Little Fawn Group Camp. The road then hooks up with the Hosmer Lake Road (described in Region Five) and campgrounds before intersecting the Cascade Lakes Highway south of Elk Lake.

Devils Lake: This is a small and rather shallow lake in a spectacular setting. **One of the youngest lava flows in Oregon** towers above the highway on the lake's northeast side. Back in the old days (before 1990) this was an unimproved car camp. The shoreline was trampled by wheeled vehicles and dotted with fire-pits and trash.

Today, cars are restricted to a nearby parking and day-use area. Campers have their choice of nine walk-in sites along the lake, ranging from a couple hundred feet from the parking area to sites a few hundred yards distant. There are vault toilets adjacent to the parking area but no water.

Region 6 — Elk Lake to Santiam Pass

Paddlers head out to explore Sparks Lake.

SPARKS LAKE RECREATION AREA INTERSECTION:
Elevation 5,460 feet.

Soda Creek Campground is the first road to our right as we enter the recreation area. There are 10 sites, and the campground can accommodate trailers to 30 feet. The campground is a fair distance from the lake proper but is adjacent to acres of beautiful meadows. There's no water here so bring your own. Next to the campground is an informational sign describing the flood on Soda Creek caused by the breach of a glacial dam on Broken Top Mountain. The road past the campground winds its way through the woods with a couple of informal campsites along the way before reaching the **Sparks Lake Day-Use Area**.

Sparks Lake: The day-use area at Sparks Lake consists of a boat launch and picnic area. The lake has no surface outlet but the porous nature of the volcanic surroundings provides the lake's water with plenty of escape points. Launch your boat and paddle close to the shore and you can find places where you can hear the water gurgling through the cracks.

The lake is shallow and by the end of the summer, the water level can fall well below the end of the paved boat ramp. When the lake

Region 6 — Elk Lake to Santiam Pass

is full and the road to the boat launch is snow free, paddlers and sailors of every description enjoy the pristine mountain scenery. With South Sister and Broken Top dominating the views to the north, the scenery here is nothing short of spectacular.

TODD LAKE / 370 ROAD INTERSECTION: Elevation 6,084 feet.

⇨ **Warning! The 370 Road is not recommended for passenger vehicles past Todd Lake Trailhead.**

South of this intersection is the **Todd Creek Horse Camp**. It's a couple of blocks to the gigantic turn-around and circle of horse camps. There's water for the stock supplied by an old fashioned hand pump but no drinking water for human critters. Designed for horse campers, the campground is usually pretty quiet in the early summer and may be available for lowly tent campers during midweek.

The road north from the intersection is suitable for any vehicle to the **Todd Lake Trailhead**. The road is gated at Todd Lake Trailhead and past the gate the road deteriorates quickly with rocks, dust, and ruts being the norm all the way to Three Creek Lake. The rough and heavily rutted road doesn't stop the adventurous from using the 370 Road to access popular hiking trails.

Due to the typically heavy snows in the Three Sisters region, the **370 Road seldom opens before August**, (August 4th in 2014). Single track with a few turn-outs, 4 to 5 miles per hour is about as fast as you can reasonably travel on the 370 Road. Just as well we can't rush through this road; some of the most spectacular scenery in the central Cascades lies ahead — my kind of road in other words.

Prior to the road opening, snowmobilers dominate this area with cross-country skiers and snowshoers playing second fiddle. Although signs are posted on the wilderness boundaries, snowmobiles regularly enter the wilderness. On one cross-country hike near Broken Top, I encountered a 12-pack of 16 oz. empties littering a remote ridge in the Three Sisters Wilderness. Why would hikers pack in 12 pounds of beer and then leave the trash here, I wondered? Then a vision of a sunny winter day with several feet of snow on the ground came to me, ah ha! Man on machine (illegal in the wilderness) was the culprit, not a thirsty hiker. Please pick up your trash!

⇦ *An artist takes the measure of Mount Bachelor, near Sparks Lake.*

Northern Oregon Backroads Guide to the PCT

MAP R6.3: TODD LAKE TO THREE CREEK LAKE

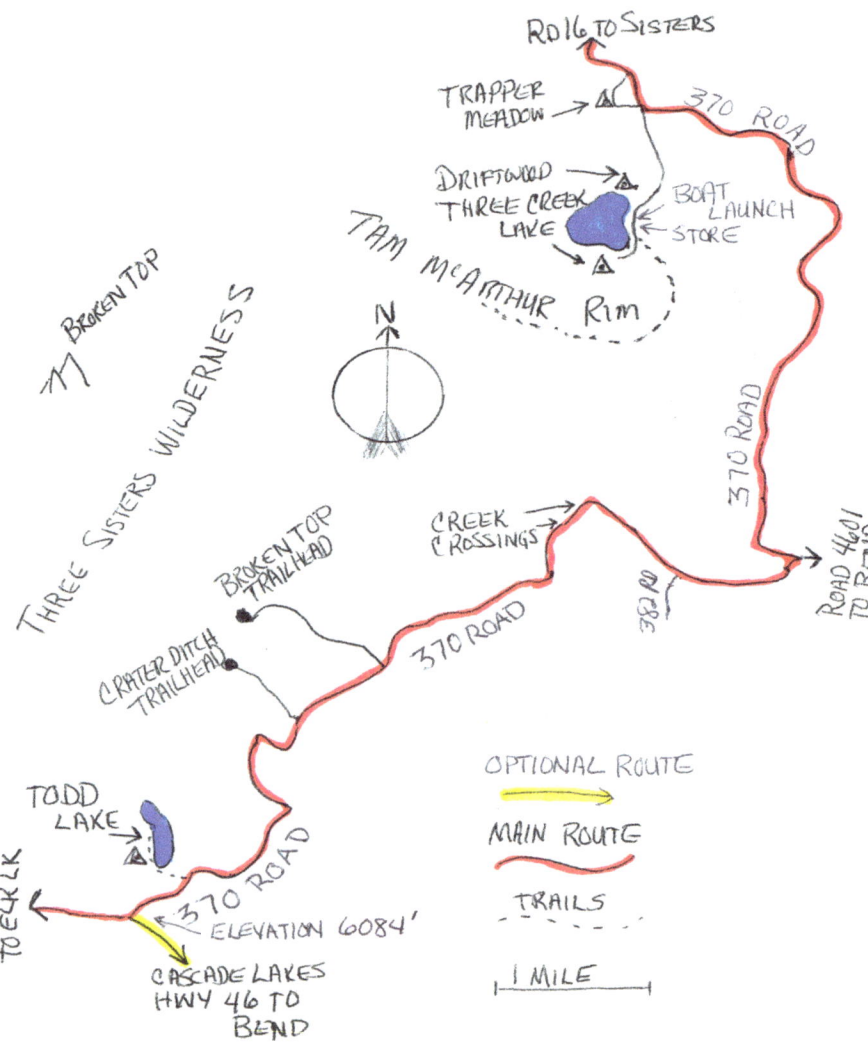

Todd Lake Day-Use Area: The parking area fills up fast on warm summer days. It's a short walk to the lake (about a city block) and the beautiful picnic area near the lake's outlet. There are vault toilets near the informational sign as the lake comes into view. Many people day hike in the area with beautiful meadows and interesting geology to explore. The rim of Broken Top peeks above the ridgeline at the lake's far end. Hike-in camping is allowed at the lake's southwestern campground.

Region 6 — Elk Lake to Santiam Pass

TODD LAKE TO SISTERS

As stated by the sign pointing out that the road you're about to drive is "Deeply Rutted," the 370 Road heads uphill through some juicy ruts as we leave the parking lot behind. We gain elevation as the road at first follows the creek uphill. After leveling out a bit, we cross through some meadow areas with views of Mount Bachelor and Broken Top in the near distance. The first road we encounter to our left after leaving Todd Lake Trailhead is the **Crater Ditch Road** leading to the Crater Ditch Trail.

Crater Ditch Road: The road follows a small stream drainage to the trailhead parking lot. Just as the name implies, the ditch trail follows a diversion ditch dug by thirsty residents and farmers in the Bend area. The trail forks ahead with the high route hooking up with the **Green Lakes Trail** and the lower way leading back to Todd Lake and Highway 46 to the south. This trail is less popular than the Broken Top Trail to the north.

BROKEN TOP: Peak elevation 9,176 feet.

Broken Top Mountain is one of the largest volcanoes in the Three Sisters realm. Once considerably taller than its present height of 9,176 feet, most of the original bulk of the mountain is now scattered about the countryside. A large amphitheater holding

A footpath leads to the Todd Lake Day-Use Area

Broken Top Mountain — A look inside a Cascade volcano reveals a layer-cake structure.

the **Crook Glacier** is all that's left of the mountain's interior and southeast side.

Built on viscous lava flows, the remnants of the stratovolcano are layered with colorful strata now exposed by the mountain's destruction. With a history of rather benign behavior, it appears that Broken Top last erupted over 100,000 years ago. Past eruptions and extensive glaciations have laid the mountain's interior bare. Looking much like Applegate Peak on the rim of Crater Lake, Broken Top's slanting summit reveals the innards of a Cascade volcano.

Gazing at the mountain from the southeast, three distinct ridges surrounding the exposed amphitheater mark the mountain's northwest side. The southern peak is known as Broken Top; the ridge marking the northern rim is known as Broken Hand; and the jagged ridge connecting the two is named St. Mary.

Broken Top Road: The road heading up to the trailhead is rugged and rocky, just like the road you've driven so far...Broken Top Trailhead is a popular place to explore the mountain's environs with many off-trail opportunities to explore for the adventurous. The trailhead, despite the rough road leading to it, is packed with hikers coming and going from the very popular Green Lakes Basin on summer weekend days. Don't

Region 6 — Elk Lake to Santiam Pass

expect solitude here during the hiking season, but show up in late September and the hordes of people are gone.

Happy Valley & Fording North Fork Tumalo Creek: After leaving the intersection at Broken Top Road, the 370 Road continues north through woods and meadows, zigging then zagging its way to a pair of creek crossings at **Happy Valley**. The first ford is usually shallow by August and September and the road climbs a shale-like shelf before wending its way to the second crossing at the bigger, Happy Valley Fork of the **North Fork Tumalo Creek**. Just past the second ford the road climbs a short, but steep and rocky hill to a campsite on your right. There's another campsite just past this one, also on the east side of the road. The adventurous can park here and get Happy, or… bushwhack your way downhill along the creek to a couple of spectacular hidden waterfalls.

The 370 Road heads sharply east after leaving the creek crossing, and in about a mile we come to a road heading downhill to our right. The short 382 Road crosses a beautiful meadow before coming to a footbridge across the North Fork Tumalo and trailhead for the 370 Trail. There are campsites here next to the creek and amid the scattered trees.

Hiking near Broken Top in the summer is very popular, but you can avoid the crowds on weekdays and after Labor Day.

Shortly after leaving the 382 Road intersection, the 370 Road comes to an intersection with the 4601 Road where we will keep left and continue north on the 370 Road to our next intersection with Forest Service Road 16 near Three Creek Lake.

FOREST ROAD 16 INTERSECTION: Elevation 6,378 feet.

The 370 Road officially ends here and if we turn left (south), we'll come to Three Creek Lake in about a mile. If we turn right (north) we immediately come to a road on the left (west), which is the entrance to Three Creek Meadow Campground. Stay on the 16 Road heading north (downhill) and we'll arrive in Sisters after about a 15-mile drive.

Three Creek Lake: Nestled below the imposing ramparts of **Tam McArthur Rim**, the lake resides at 6,500 feet in elevation. It's a popular fishery, perhaps for the stunning beauty of the setting as much as the fishing. This is snow country with the massifs of the Three Sisters and Broken Top Mountains to our east creating their own weather. With hundreds of inches of snow expected to fall in a typical year, the 16 Road from the town of Sisters to the lake is typically closed by snow and gated from November until early July.

Vibrant paintbrush colors the landscape along Tumalo Creek.

Region 6 — Elk Lake to Santiam Pass

Looking north from Tam McArthur Rim, hikers take a break.

Two snow parks are located along the 16 Road, with the area around Three Creek Lake and Broken Top popular with snowmobilers in the snowy season. Even early summer can be cold at these elevations so come prepared if you're planning to camp here any time of the year. Two campgrounds are at the lake; neither have water.

Driftwood Campground is to our right as we approach the lake. A parking area and a short trail lead to the rustic, walk-in campsites strung along the lake. A foot trail leads from Driftwood Campground and arrives at Little Three Creek Lake in less than a mile.

Three Creek Campground is snug below the Rim on the south side of the lake and has 10 sites with tables, fire rings, and toilets. This is where the road ends so expect to watch a lot of people turning around if you camp here.

Tam McArthur Rim: The hike to the rim overlook is listed as 2.6 miles (5.2 miles round-trip) and begins at Three Creek Lake. The trail heads up quickly and crosses a steep, rocky outcrop. The views begin almost immediately with snow-capped mountains in the background and the lake nearby. The tread switches back as it heads upward and the views to the north open up; be careful not to take one of a couple dead-end side trails forking off the main trail as you gawk at the scenery.

Northern Oregon Backroads Guide to the PCT

Mother Nature has shown us the extreme side of her personality in past seasons with drought and fires. Recent years have been warm with less snow than average in the high country of Oregon. Some big fires have gotten loose in the country to our north with the **Pole Creek Fire of September 2012** being the most significant locally. As the trail leaves the lake, views to the north open up, and we begin to see the scope of the fire's devastation stretching towards the town of Sisters.

After gaining some sweat-inducing altitude, the way heads westerly in earnest with more views as it meets the rim's edge. The path heads straight uphill in pumice soil before making its way to the "Prow" of Tam McArthur Rim and the end of the formal trail.

The views of the snow-capped volcanoes marching to the northern horizon are superb on a clear day. Gaze directly off the edge of the sheer cliff to a helicopter-like view of **Little Three Creek Lake**. More miles of high country adventure are off the formal trail. Head westerly past the viewpoint further along the rim and get up close and personal with Broken Top's northern side amidst more mountain wandering.

The 16 Road to Sisters: As we head north and downhill on the paved 16 Road from Three Creek Lake, we come to a major intersection to our left marking the entrance to Three Creek Meadows Campground.

Three Creek Meadows Campground: As you might expect, the campground spreads across a beautiful meadow area. This is the place you'll usually find the larger motorhome campers and horse trailers. There are great views of the "Prow" of Tam McArthur Ridge from every campsite. There are 11 sites and no drinking water.

Whychus Creek: (Pronounced *WHY-chuse*) The creek that parallels our descent towards Sisters was once known as Squaw Creek; the name was changed to Whychus in 2006. The meaning of Whychus in the native Sahaptin language translates to "water crossing," perhaps a shallow ford or bridge across a creek or river. Regardless of what you call it, Whychus is a beautiful stream with a huge drainage heading into the heart of the Sisters Wilderness and running into the Deschutes River several miles northeast of Sisters. Dispersed camping is allowed in the drainage.

Recent efforts have led to the removal of the last private dam on the Whychus and now the creek runs free once again. Local landowners and fishing groups have been working together to restore riparian areas and historic fish runs in the upper Whychus drainage.

Region 6 — Elk Lake to Santiam Pass

MAP R6.4: SISTERS TO SANTIAM PASS

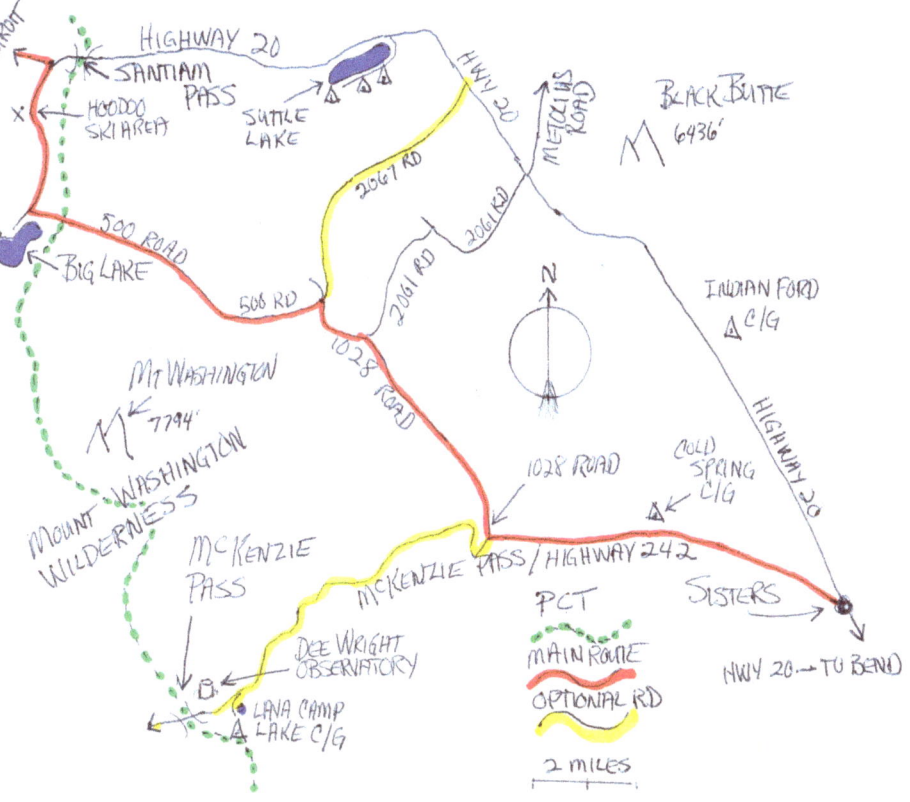

To further explore Whychus Creek, take the 1514 Road from Forest Road 16 as we approach Sisters and head west about 3 miles to the creek.

SISTERS TO SANTIAM PASS

It's tempting to say the town of Sisters is mostly about traffic. On summer weekends there is a near gridlock feel to downtown with giant motor homes and trucks inching through town as pedestrians dodge distracted drivers. Santiam Pass (18 miles west of town) is a natural low spot through the Cascades and has been used by travelers for thousands of years to connect the Willamette Valley to the high desert country of Central Oregon.

But there's more to this place than diesel fumes and gesturing drivers. In sharp contrast to the summertime chaos in town are the stunning Three Sisters themselves. Named **Hope, Faith,** and **Charity,**

Tourists, traffic, and colorful knick-knacks abound in Sisters.

the volcanoes gracing the skyline to the southwest are the town's namesakes. Other mountains poke their heads up nearby including **Three Fingered Jack** and **Mount Jefferson** to the northwest. All of these snow-covered volcanoes are surrounded by many square miles of wilderness, promising peace and quiet to those who seek it. Those drawn to this place are people who value the wild country in their own backyards. The Deschutes National Forest borders the town and the ranger station in Sisters is a good source for local maps and information.

Sisters: Founded shortly after 1900, Sisters became the hub for the local ranching and lumber industries. Falling on hard times after the last of the lumber mills closed in the 1960s, Sisters became little more than a wide spot in the road. Always endowed with scenic beauty, the town was rediscovered by outdoors lovers and later adopted a western architectural theme to lure travelers along the highway to stop and explore. If the lack of parking around town is any measure, Sisters has successfully persuaded many travelers to take a look around.

Today the town has an attractive downtown and a variety of small shops catering to the tourist trade. Area restaurants scattered about town offer menu items from fast food to upscale cuisine at the nearby

Region 6 — Elk Lake to Santiam Pass

Black Butte Ranch. For great Mexican-style food visit **Los Agaves Restaurant**. Located on the eastern end of the main drag, Los Agaves presents all of their dishes with a flair not normally found in reasonably priced family Mexican restaurants. They also have a pleasant patio alongside the main dining area and a full bar.

Sisters hosts several events throughout the year including the **Sisters Folk Festival**. Held in early September, the festival has turned into a huge event and attracts many talented roots musicians and fans from all over North America. The festival is spread out at various venues around town, and festival-goers can walk from place to place. The music ranges from soul-stirring blues to get up and dance bluegrass and Celtic tunes. Lodging in or near Sisters is impossible during the Folk Festival so plan well in advance if you want to attend. The Folkfest celebrated its 20th year in 2015. For more information look at sistersfolkfestival.org.

Advertised as the biggest outdoor quilt display in the country with well over 1,000 on display around town, the **Sisters Outdoor Quilt Show** is held in July. Colorful quilts splash color across town during this display, weather permitting. Bring your camera and take a stroll around Sisters to admire the artistry of master quilters. Another noteworthy show held in July is the **Round-Up of Gems** displaying rocks and minerals for sale. It was held over the Fourth of July weekend in 2014.

"The Biggest Little Show in the World," the **Sisters Rodeo**, is a four-day party. Held in early June each year, the rodeo draws huge crowds; the Sisters Rodeo grounds are about three miles east of town on Highway 20. This big-time rodeo event attracts fans to watch professional cowboys and cowgirls compete in events from bull riding to barrel racing. A popular and colorful parade is held downtown on Cascade Avenue, Saturday morning of the rodeo. Call 1-800-827-7522 for rodeo tickets.

Throw in a few more shows sprinkled throughout the summer and fall seasons like the **Glory Daze Car Show**, the **Sisters Fresh Hops Festival**, the **Harvest Faire**, and several more and it begins to feel like Sisters is on the verge of being loved to death…It's easy to see why traffic gets snarly through town.

Some of these events draw big crowds and create big traffic headaches. If you choose to spend time in town during the summer or fall and want to avoid the masses, opt for a (rare) weekend with nothing (huge) scheduled in town.

MCKENZIE PASS HIGHWAY

> **Warning: The high elevation portion of the McKenzie Pass Hwy. is closed to vehicles or combinations exceeding 35 feet at all times. The upper highway is not plowed and is gated from November to July in most years.**

As we drive west through the outskirts of Sisters on Highway 20, look for the exit signs directing you to McKenzie Pass / Highway 242. The McKenzie Pass Highway splits off from Highway 20 and heads due west from Sisters. After leaving town the highway quickly enters the national forest and after driving 3.7 miles west, we encounter Cold Spring Campground.

COLD SPRING CAMPGROUND: Elevation 3,341 feet

Cold Spring brings the gift of life to this normally dry part of the eastern Cascades. Popular with birders and (birds too) springtime brings both to wander about the wooded riparian area adjacent to the campground. Expect to see kinglets, woodpeckers, and sapsuckers inhabiting the woods along the lovely creek. Many wildflowers grow in these moist environs, watch for hummingbirds working the nectar in the spring and early summer. The campground has 23 sites, vault toilets, and water.

Intersection of the 1028 Road: We head north on the improved gravel 1028 Road to our intersection with the Old Santiam Pass Wagon Road – Road 500.

> **Special Note:** *I highly recommend the optional McKenzie Pass Highway (described at the beginning of this chapter) for further exploration. The road is extremely narrow where it has been cut through the solid lava rock covering the summit and vehicles longer than 35 feet are restricted at all times. Personally I wouldn't want to drive anything much bigger than a pickup to the summit. If your load is light and the weather is good, make the drive to Dee Wright Observatory; you won't regret it. Add at least an hour to your time if you choose to explore the McKenzie Pass area.*

The riparian area along Cold Spring Creek attracts birds and birders.

Northern Oregon Backroads Guide to the PCT

Along the 500 Road: This is the old Santiam Wagon Road and edges along the Three Sisters Wilderness area as it makes its way to Big Lake Campground.

⇨ **Warning, not suitable for passenger cars.**

Several areas have been washed out, ranking anywhere from mildly washed to deeply rutted and muddy in the early season. **Four-wheel drive is recommended.** The other alternative to muddy seems to be dusty with little in between — no doubt the same conditions the wagoners faced before the auto age. Take your time and enjoy the views of Mount Washington to the south.

The devastating **B&B Fire of 2003** burned huge swaths of the Three Sisters Wilderness and the adjoining National Forest. This fire burned for weeks and was largely out of the control of man. Years of fire suppression had led to big fuel loads and when the fire got a good start, little could be done more than standing back and watching her go. The rains of fall and the snows of winter finally extinguished the monster but not before many square miles of timber were devastated.

This fire (like all forest fires) presented both good and bad news for the forest communities. From our point of view we see little beyond the scorched earth, at least initially. The high elevation and

Along the 500 Road, deep-rooted pussypaws are among the first to return after forest fires.

Region 6 — Elk Lake to Santiam Pass

pumiceous nature of the volcanic soil make growing conditions difficult at best for plants and animals colonizing the burned areas. Nonetheless, life insists on moving back in.

Early summer brings a copious blossoming of bear grass, swaying in the breeze. Wildflowers of every description inhabit the burned-over slopes, from lupine to shooting stars. Trees are slowly filling in the spaces created by the fire and now survive summer drought and winter flattening.

We intersect the **Pacific Crest Trail along the 500 Road shortly before we come to Big Lake** and the end of the 500 Road at the intersection of the 2690 Road.

> ⇨ **Note:** Just before the intersection with the 2690 Road, we glimpse a shallow arm of Big Lake adjacent to the 500 Road. There's a channel of the lake very close to the road and it would be feasible to slide a paddle craft into the water here.

2690 Road Intersection:

> ⇨ **Special Note:** If we follow the 2690 Road north we pass the Hoodoo Ski Bowl before arriving at Santiam Pass and the end of Region Six.

If we turn left (south) at this intersection we immediately arrive at the entrance to **Big Lake Campground**.

Deep rooted Pussy Paws, *Calyptridium umbellatum*, are among the first wild flowers to appear after a forest fire. The stout root can extend ten or more feet in pumice soils found in the central Cascades of Oregon. The flowers have the velvety feel of fur and often form a circle around the leaf rosettes.

BIG LAKE: Elevation 4,660 feet at the surface.

Covering over 220 acres, Big Lake offers fishermen the opportunity to hook a variety of fish including kokanee, rainbow, cutthroat and brook trout. The elevation and location near the top of the Cascade Range means cold and windy conditions anytime of the year. Come prepared for the weather if you're planning on fishing or camping here. There's a youth camp on the southeast side but no commercial development on the lake.

Campgrounds at Big Lake: Two campgrounds are at Big Lake; both sites have drinking water. **Big Lake Campground** has 49 sites and is located on a loop along the northwest side of the lake. There's a boat launch near the entrance of the campground with a paved ramp.

Big Lake West has 11 sites and is laid out in a linear fashion with parking along the road and a short walk to the picnic tables and individual campsites.

Santiam Pass, Highway 20, and the beginning of Region Seven are about 3.5 miles north of Big Lake on the 2690 Road. We pass the Hoodoo Ski Bowl before reaching the highway.

END OF REGION SIX

Region Six, starting at Elk Lake, has taken us through some of the most beautiful high country available to motorists in Oregon. Staying on the east side (the dry side) of the divide, Region Six roads are more open, with bigger vistas than most byways through Oregon's forests. The presence of the massive volcanoes in the Sisters Wilderness is a palpable thing for those on the Pacific Crest Trail and wheeled travelers alike.

In Region Seven we'll be almost exclusively on the west (wet) side of the Cascade Divide. Bigger trees grow in this rainier climate and drape the slopes of the volcanoes to our north, birthplaces of famous rivers in Oregon lore. The waters of the Santiam River guide us to Detroit Lake where we head uphill again, along the Breitenbush River to its source at Breitenbush Lake and our next meeting with the Pacific Crest Trail.

Mount Washington lies to the south of Big Lake Campground and the end of Region Six.

MAP R7.1: MAIN ROUTE

REGION SEVEN
Santiam Pass to Olallie Lake

Sahalie Falls cascades more than 70 feet into the McKenzie River.

THE JOURNEY NOT FORGOTTEN

The question, "What lies ahead?" is an old one,
Pondered by travelers from our misty past.
What promise does the land hold?
Which way shall we go?

Ancient memories still Guide us.
Mountains to climb and Rivers to ford;
Our discoveries fill us with wonder on this
Journey not forgotten.

Region 7 — Santiam Pass to Olallie Lake

ROUTE DESCRIPTION

The Main Route heads west on Highway 20 from Santiam Pass. On our way to the turn-off at Santiam Junction we'll pass Lost Lake and Lost Lake Campground. At Santiam Junction we have the option of taking a side trip to Sahalie Falls.

From Santiam Junction the Main Route heads north on Highway 22 to our turn-off at Big Meadows Road. After passing Big Meadows Campground, we'll cross the North Santiam River before arriving at Fay Lake. From Fay Lake we'll follow the rough 2257 Road as we edge along the Mount Jefferson Wilderness before arriving again at Highway 22. After exploring the Santiam River and the town of Detroit Lake, we'll head northeast on Forest Highway 46 following the Breitenbush River to our next turn at Breitenbush Lake Road. We'll follow the very rugged 4220 Road (not suitable for passenger cars) to Breitenbush Lake. From there we make our way north to Olallie Lake Resort and the end of Region Seven.

> **Note:** *The scenic 4220 Road (also known as the "Oregon Skyline Road") connecting Breitenbush and Olallie Lakes is short but extremely rough; it's slow going in any vehicle. Plan on at least 2 hours to drive the rugged 4220 Road from the pavement end at Forest Highway 46 to Olallie Lake Resort. The section of the 4220 Road connecting Breitenbush Lake with Olallie Lake is blocked by snow in typical years until early summer.*

> *The optional (for low clearance vehicles) paved Forest Highway 46 and the connecting 4690 Road to Olallie Lake from the north will take the driver about 1.5 hours from Detroit Lake to Olallie Lake Resort.*

ROAD CONDITIONS

The route is mostly paved with the exception of the 2257 Road past Fay Lake and the Breitenbush Lake / 4220 Road. Low-clearance vehicles should avoid these two roads and take the optional routes described below.

RECOMMENDED MAPS FOR REGION SEVEN

Both the Willamette Cascades and Detroit area maps are available at the Detroit Lake Ranger Station at Detroit Lake. Call 541-844-3566

⇐ *Mount Jefferson, elevation 10,497 feet.*

Northern Oregon Backroads Guide to the PCT

or order maps online at fs.fed.us/r6/willamette. Benchmark maps are available at book stores, sporting goods stores, and on-line at benchmarkmaps.com.

- *Willamette Cascades Forest Recreation Map*
- *Detroit Ranger District Map*
- Benchmark Maps – *Oregon Road and Recreation Atlas*, pages 61 and 49.

OPTIONAL ROUTES & ROADS IN REGION SEVEN

You must avoid two roads in Region Seven if you're driving a low-clearance vehicle:

1. The 2257 Road connecting Fay Lake to Marion Forks is rough and has clearance issues. To avoid this rough road, stay on Highway 22 from Santiam Junction to Marion Forks.

2. The 4220 Road connecting Breitenbush Lake with Olallie Lake is very gnarly and definitely **not suited to passenger vehicles**. To avoid the rough part of the 4220 Road, drive the 46 Road, north, to its intersection with the 4690 Road (refer to Map R7.1). Drive east on the 4690 Road to its intersection with the 4220 Road and follow the 4220 Road south to Olallie Lake Resort. The 4220 Road from this intersection is navigable by passenger cars to Olallie Lake Resort with caution.

The other optional road (described below) is a side trip to Sahalie and Koosah Falls ('cause we all love waterfalls, mountain lakes, and history, right?) and an exploration of the Clear Lake area. Allow at least an extra hour and a half to explore the lakes and waterfalls. It would be easy to spend 3 to 4 hours exploring this rather compact stretch of Highway 126. This optional side-trip route is paved.

Optional Side-Trip to Sahalie Falls Area: From Santiam Junction we'll stay left and drive west on Highway 20 for about 2.5 miles to the junction with Highway 126. From that intersection we'll head south (left) on Highway 126. As we drive south on Highway 126, we'll see the Three Sisters poking their heads above the lava fields next to the road. First up on the Highway 126 "hit parade" is the Fish Lake Remount Depot.

Fish Lake Remount Depot: The sign on the west side of the highway says Fish Lake G.S. (Guard Station). A small parking area marks the trailhead to the depot. The Fish Lake Remount Depot

Region 7 — Santiam Pass to Olallie Lake

The Fish Lake Remount Station is still used by packers hired by the Forest Service.

stands at an altitude of nearly 3,200 feet in the Willamette National Forest. Two rustic cabins are for rent here from December to April 15th. Accessed by walking, skiing, or snowshoeing about 0.75 miles from the parking area on Highway 126, the cabins were built in 1924 and include a dispatcher's cabin and associated structures and another larger cabin with two bedrooms. The two-bedroom cabin and the dispatcher's cabin, known as the Hall House, are available as rentals either separately or together.

Each cabin is furnished with basic housekeeping items along with propane heating and cooking stoves. There is no electricity or water at either cabin, so you must bring plenty of water for yourselves. Sno-park permits are required during snow season if you leave your car at the highway. The depot is still used as a rest and resupply station by Forest Service horse-packers heading in and out of nearby wilderness areas in the warmer months. See the Forest Service's website for costs and availability.

Back on the highway heading south, the next point of interest is the Fish Lake Day-Use Area.

Fish Lake Day-Use Area: The Remount Depot rental cabins can also be accessed by a trail from the Fish Lake Day-Use Area but the distance is about the same. The day-use area has informational signs near the shallow lake explaining how **Fish Lake becomes a large grassy meadow** in most years. Picnic tables and vault toilets are adjacent to the turnaround. From the parking lot, the re-created wagon road toll-gates lead the walker to the nearby Remount Station and another display detailing the interesting history of the **Santiam Pass Wagon Road** and Fish Lake's role in the development and operation of the old road.

McKenzie River Trail: Feel like taking a stroll? The river trail is about 27 miles long and is popular with hikers and mountain bikers. In fact (for better or worse), a nationally distributed mountain biker magazine named this trail as the best mountain biking trail in the United States. The trail begins in the north at Fish Lake and ends near the Ranger Station at McKenzie Bridge. Mostly downhill north to south, the trail leads past dramatic waterfalls and rapids along the McKenzie with many swimming holes and access points to the road along the way.

Clear Lake Area: The waters of Clear Lake are clear. No...I mean REALLY clear — gin clear, as the fisher person might tell you. Like many lakes in Oregon's High Cascades, the cold, lava-lined waters

Ancient tree stumps are preserved in the crystalline depths of Clear Lake. These 3,000-year-old relics date from the lake's formation.

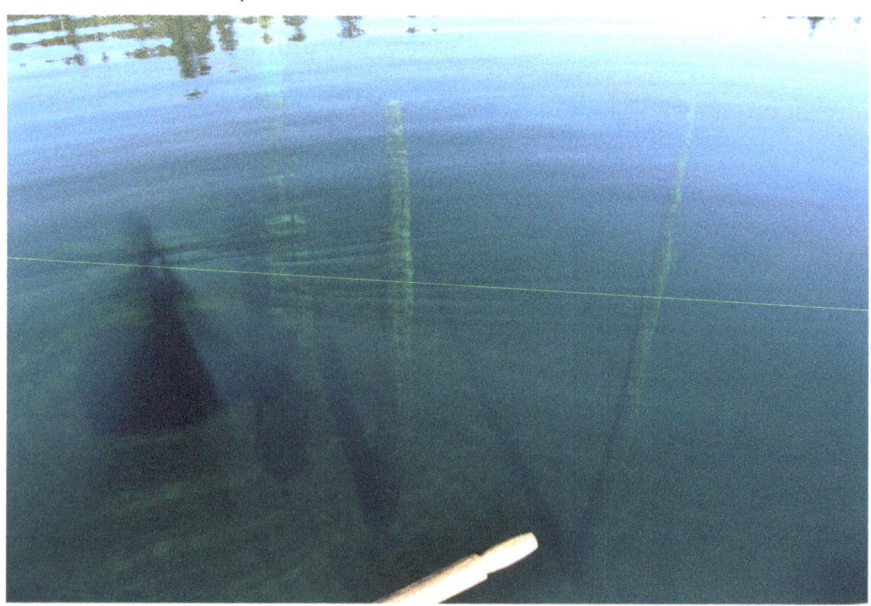

Region 7 — Santiam Pass to Olallie Lake

Stunning Koosah Falls plunges more than 60 feet into the McKenzie River.

contain few nutrients for growing algae and other food chain basics. Despite the tough conditions a fair population of brook trout and a few cutthroat inhabit the lake, and it's stocked seasonally with rainbows, some of which grow quite large. The transparent waters can make for frustrating fishing with the fish mostly seeing you before you can eye them. All methods are used to catch fish but still-fishing and trolling are most popular.

The deep lake was formed quite recently (in geological terms) by a lava flow across the McKenzie River **only about 3,000 years ago**. The deep, icy waters of the lake have preserved a grove of trees that date from that age and can be seen, trunks still standing, in the lake's crystalline depths. The McKenzie River heads above the lake at Great Spring, but the lake is generally recognized as the source of the mighty McKenzie River.

Clear Lake Resort is located along the northwest side of the 150-acre lake and rents rowboats and cabins. A small store and grill are located at the lodge (the cafe part of the operation kicks off on Mother's Day), and the resort is open year-round. The road down to the resort from Highway 126 is narrow and winding and can be icy during the winter; plan on using four-wheel drive to climb the hill when it's slick and even chains when it's snow-packed.

The marina rents rowboats or you can bring your own paddle craft, no motors are allowed on the lake. In days gone by, you could rent a wooden rowboat at the marina. These "living" boats were heavy, stable, and somewhat leaky but didn't get blown around by the wind and were easy to enter and exit from the dock. They also required more maintenance than a fiberglass or aluminum boat. Alas, the wooden boats have been dragged out of the water and aluminum boats are lined up at the dock these days; careful getting in and out of these tipsy craft. The resort charges $5.00 to use their launch if you're launching your own boat. The wind can kick up on this high lake, especially in the afternoon. If you're caught on the south end of the lake with the wind blowing hard, it can be a long row back to the resort in your skittery vessel.

The cabins are arrayed in a loop along the shore north of the lodge. I stayed in one of the Modern Cabins featuring two bedrooms with queen beds, propane heat and stove, and a bathroom with shower. Bring your own bedding, linens, soap, and utensils for cooking and eating. Electricity is supplied by a generator and may be limited during the winter season.

Cold Water Cove Campground is located on the southeast side of the lake and connects to Highway 126 via a short paved road. Laid out on a loop, about a third of the 35 campsites are close to the lake. There's pump-handle water at the campground with accessible vault toilets. A **foot trail leads around the lake** and the part crossing the lava field below the campground is paved and leads to a bench with a nice view of the lake. The campground does not have a boat launch, but it's possible to find a few spots to slip a small craft into the water.

Sahalie and Koosah Falls: Perhaps the most beautiful waterfalls in the central Oregon Cascades, the full force of the McKenzie River plunges over a 73-foot ledge into the splash pool below **Sahalie Falls**. The informational signs at the parking lot kiosk tell the dramatic geological story of Sahalie and Koosah Falls just below us. The walk from the parking lot to the Sahalie viewing area is a couple of hundred feet at best. This most impressive of the McKenzie River falls was formed by lava flows from the **Belknap Crater** to our east.

Follow the trail downhill past the Sahalie viewing area to a dramatic perch at the top of 64-foot-tall Koosah Falls. Continue south along

Region 7 — Santiam Pass to Olallie Lake

the trail to more views from below the falls with some railings providing just enough room for two to ogle the incredible scene. The trail heads downhill to Ice Cap Campground and the parking area for Koosah Falls.

This is the end of the side trip description. Highway 126 follows the McKenzie River downhill (south) from here. Belknap Hot Springs and the town of McKenzie Bridge are about 12 miles south of the Sahalie Falls parking lot.

PCT ACCESS POINTS

Three points access the PCT in Region Seven.
1. The PCT trailhead at Santiam Pass is accessed via a short road leading north from Highway 20. From Santiam Pass to Breitenbush Lake, it is 40 trail miles.
2. The next road access is at Breitenbush Lake. From Breitenbush Lake to Olallie Lake Resort, it's 6.5 trail miles.
3. The PCT crosses the road at Olallie Lake Resort and the end of Region Seven.

MAIN ROADS IN ORDER OF TRAVEL

All road descriptions are South to North.

Oregon Highway 20	We're on this road for a few miles to Santiam Junction.
Oregon Highway 22	From Santiam Junction we'll head north to the Big Meadows / 2267 Road.
Big Meadows / 2267 Road	We're on this road for only a mile when we turn on the 2257 Road.
2257 Road	The road to Fay Lake and northward to an intersection with Highway 22 near Marion Forks. Rough road beyond Fay Lake.
Highway 22	We're back on 22 to the town of Detroit Lake. From the lake we'll head north on Forest Highway 46.
Forest Highway 46	We follow this road along the Breitenbush River to our next turn at the 4220 Road.
4220 Road (also called the Skyline Road)	This is the rough road to Breitenbush Lake and beyond to Olallie Lake Resort and the end of Region Seven.

Northern Oregon Backroads Guide to the PCT

MAP R7.2: SANTIAM JUNCTION & SAHALIE FALLS

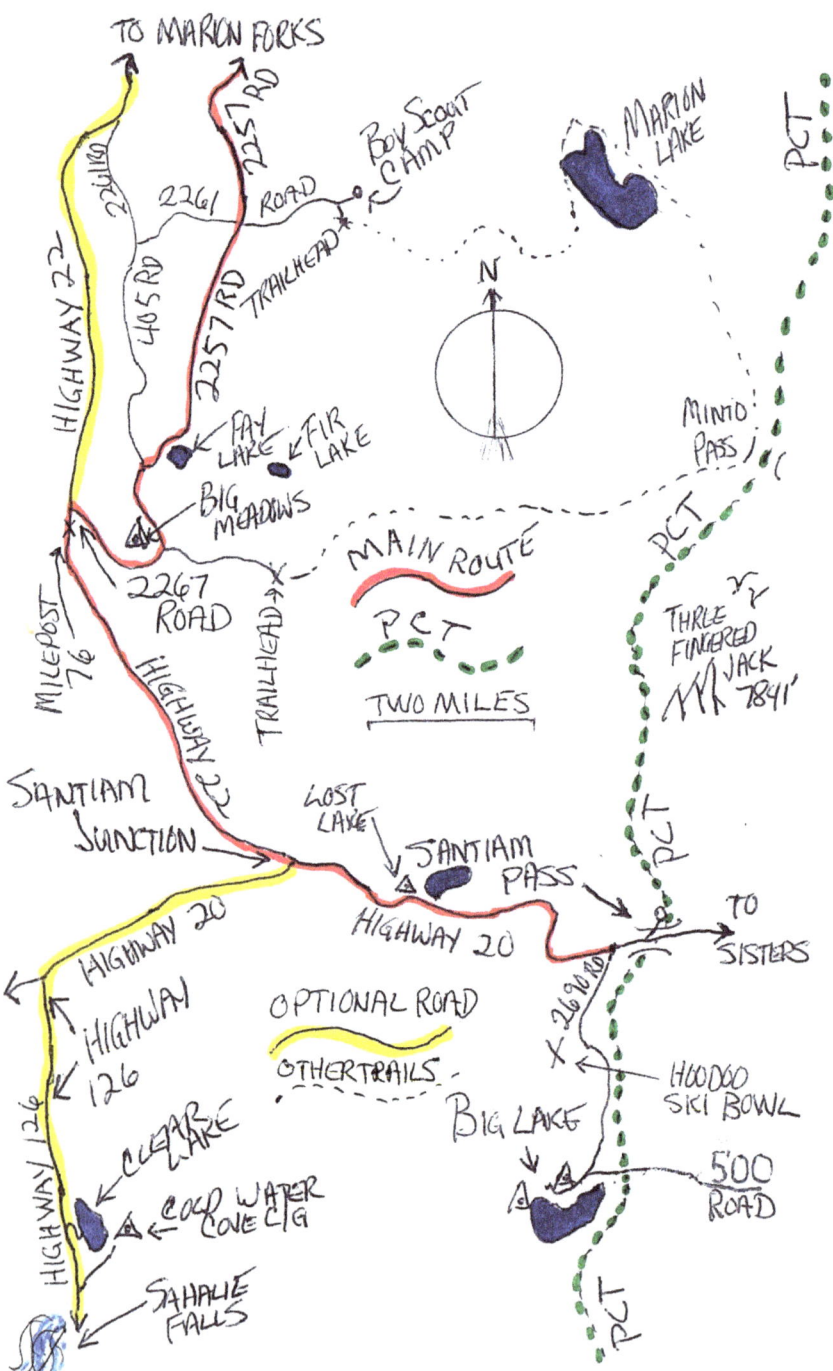

Region 7 — Santiam Pass to Olallie Lake

Looking south from Santiam Pass, Mount Washington is in the distance.

ROAD NOTES – REGION SEVEN

Santiam Pass is where we begin the Main Route through Region Seven, first heading toward Santiam Junction.

SANTIAM PASS: Elevation 4,187 feet.

Highway 20 heads west from Santiam Pass immediately going downhill and curving to the right around **Hogg Rock** (more about Mr. Thomas Egeton Hogg later) presenting the driver with a dramatic view of heavily eroded Three Fingered Jack, looming to the north.

Hogg Rock, like Hayrick Mountain to the south, is interesting geologically. Known as a **Tuya Volcano**, Hogg Rock is one of the best known examples of the results of a sub-glacial eruption. Rising steep-sided, the walls of the volcano tell a story. As the lava and gases caused by the eruption about 80,000 years ago melted their way through the massive ice-field above, the tremendous pressure of the surrounding ice constricted the newborn mountain's lateral spread. Lava pooling on top formed the flat top we see today. The term Tuya is derived from a region of similar steep-sided formations in northern British Columbia, Canada. This type of volcano is fairly rare in the world; seldom does heavy ice cover ongoing volcanic eruptions.

Northern Oregon Backroads Guide to the PCT

Take it easy as you head west down the highway; the curve to the left is sharp and the traffic can be in a hurry. When the road straightens out, look for the turn to **Lost Lake Campground** on your right. This version of "Lost Lake" is among about 20 Lost Lakes in Oregon and among thousands in North America. Lost Lake is extremely shallow and virtually disappears (truly lost!) in dry years. The campground is rambling and has some informal sites in the woods nearby. Vault toilets and a few picnic tables mark the campground. After leaving the lake, Highway 20 arrives quickly at Santiam Junction.

SANTIAM JUNCTION: Elevation 3,750 feet.

A public airport at the junction allows fly-in camping. The airstrip is behind the highway maintenance buildings.

Decision time at Santiam Junction: Keep to the right on **Highway 22 to Detroit Lake**, following the Main Route north, or...

If you wish to take the **optional side-trip** (described above) to Sahalie and Koosah Falls, then **turn left and follow Highway 20** about 2.5 miles to its intersection with Highway 126. After turning south, follow Highway 126 towards Clear Lake.

HIGHWAY 22 NORTH TO DETROIT LAKE

From Santiam Junction the Main Route heads north through fields of lava laid down about 3,000 years ago. Highway 22 begins to head downhill, and if the guy behind you doesn't really care about the scenery and is in a hurry, be sure to pull over where you can to let him pass by. Look for mileposts on the opposite side of the road and pay attention when you get to **milepost 76**. The turn-off to **Big Meadows Road** comes up quickly at milepost 76.

BIG MEADOWS / 2267 ROAD: Elevation 3,521 feet.

Look for this road at milepost 76. Head right (east) on the paved 2267 Road for a mile to the intersection of the 2257 Road where we'll turn north onto the 2257 Road.

Heading North on the 2257 Road: It's a nice half-mile drive through the big trees and lush forest on the one-lane (with turn-outs) paved road to reach the horse camp on our left.

Big Meadows Horse Camp: Some horse camps are more welcome to car campers than others, and this one is quiet enough to probably not offend the horse crowd before hunting season. If you don't mind the smell of composting horse poo (and you're not one of those evil

Region 7 — Santiam Pass to Olallie Lake

Found near the North Santiam, this Amanita rubescens, *recognized by its cup-shaped bulb, is a member of the extensive Amanita family.*

mountain bikers) the campsites are huge with corrals and loading ramps in case you need those facilities.

If you're a horse camping person (and you know who you are) this is a nice place in the spring before the skeeters get pesky and again in the fall when the bugs and tourists have slackened and the snow in the high country is gone. Laid out in a circle, it's a good place to round up the wagons. There is a pump handle for water and vault toilets. Many trails radiate from here, heading uphill and following ways to mountain lakes and the Pacific Crest Trail at Minto Pass.

Back on the 2257 Road Heading North: After leaving the campground the paved road stays on level ground, and in less than a quarter-mile we come to the bridged crossing of the **North Fork Santiam River**. Though the title is long, the North Fork Santiam River at this point is just a good-sized creek most of the year. Possible camps are at the river crossing and along the way. A wide spot on the right before crossing the bridge provides easy water access for your furry friends. Look around the riparian area adjacent to the stream for mushrooms and other water loving plants and animals.

Amanita rubescens, "the blusher," is often found near the North Santiam River. This mushroom reddens where cut or bruised. Other

Northern Oregon Backroads Guide to the PCT

Snow-covered Mount Jefferson crowds the horizon from the 2261 Road, a short side-trip from the 2257/Fay Lake Road.

members of the Amanita family are responsible for the majority of fatal mushroom poisonings in North America. All members of the extensive Amanita mushroom family are recognized by the cup-shaped bulb (vulva) from which they grow.

After leaving the bridge, we follow the paved road just over a mile to the end of pavement and the **intersection with the 405 Road**. The 405 Road is an improved gravel road. **Many people seeking Fay Lake mistakenly take this road.**

The **dirt 2257 Road heads uphill** from this intersection and immediately comes to a "Y" with the way to the right leading to a gated trailhead with no turnaround. Stay left and continue uphill along the 2257 Road another 0.3 miles to Fay Lake.

<u>FAY LAKE:</u> Elevation 3,950 feet.

Fay Lake covers 8 or 9 acres and is surrounded by trees. A few informal campsites with no amenities are located along the road. If you're looking for a lakefront campsite on a quiet lake, this could be for you. This is a brook trout lake (with a few rainbows in the mix) that's hard to fish from the brushy shore; bring an inflatable or small boat to effectively fish here.

Region 7 — Santiam Pass to Olallie Lake

Back on the 2257 Road Heading North: The road gets somewhat worse as we leave Fay Lake and heads north with rocks and potholes; take it slow and in only a quarter-mile past Fay we come to the trailhead for **Pika** and **Fir Lakes**.

Fir Lake has a reputation for being an excellent lake for fishing with some brook trout reportedly to 18 inches. For years it was a boot-beaten path through disorienting brush to reach Fir, but now a formal Trail #3489 is well established to these lakes. It's about a half-mile to tiny Pika Lake and another half-mile past that to much deeper and bigger Fir Lake.

Leaving the trailhead, the 2257 Road continues rough and slow going; it's about 3.5 miles north to the intersection with the paved 2261 Road. Take it on the slow side and enjoy the fact you'll not be ticketed for speeding.

INTERSECTION OF THE 2261 ROAD: Elevation 3,492 feet.

The 2261 Road heads east and uphill to the Boy Scout's Camp Pioneer and a trailhead to Pine Ridge. Just 0.6 miles uphill from the intersection takes you to a nice viewpoint of Mount Jefferson's southwest face.

Drive through Marion Forks Hatchery like you own it to reach the small campground beyond.

Northern Oregon Backroads Guide to the PCT

Continuing North on the 2257 Road: From the 2261 Road intersection, the 2257 Road continues on the rough side for another 2.0 miles before getting better. Another half-mile past that we come to a three-way intersection with the 2257 Road becoming paved at this point and the gravel 515 Road heading southeast.

Head up the 515 Road about a half-mile and you'll see shallow **Presley Lake** on the north side of the road. A short, rough spur road heads down to the lake and a couple of rough campsites.

Heading north on the paved 2257 Road, the views towards Mount Jefferson start to open up before we head down Pine Ridge, 2.6 miles to our **intersection with Highway 22**. Turning right (north) on Highway 22 we'll drive less than a quarter-mile before encountering the Marion Forks Fish Hatchery and Campground on our right.

Marion Forks Fish Hatchery & Campground: I hesitate to tell anyone about this campground. Just far enough off the highway to be shielded from the hum of Highway 22, this quiet little spot offers few amenities for the Winnebago crowd. There's not much room to maneuver behemoth trailers and motor homes and there's little advertisement of its existence from the highway.

The turn-off to the right (east) from the high speed highway comes up abruptly. Look for the turn marking the Marion Forks Fish Hatchery between the stretches of guard rails. Driving into the fish hatchery you might think you've taken the wrong turn, but drive through the place like you own it and look for the campground sign at the end of the hatchery grounds. It does not have a lot to offer a family for a stay-cation at the campground but there are miles and miles of trails in the area. It's mostly day-hikers who stumble across this camp and make it headquarters for exploring the west side of the **Mount Jefferson Wilderness**.

There's just enough room to park your camper or small trailer but this site is best suited for car campers. There is no place to get water in the campground (perhaps the fish hatchery has potable water?) so bring your own. **Riverside Campground is two miles north** along Highway 22 and has water.

WHITEWATER ROAD: Elevation at the Highway 2,182 feet.

> ⇨ **Note:** *The Whitewater Road is not part of the Main Route. See Map R.7.1*

Region 7 — Santiam Pass to Olallie Lake

MAP R7.3: EASTERN PORTION OF DETROIT LAKE

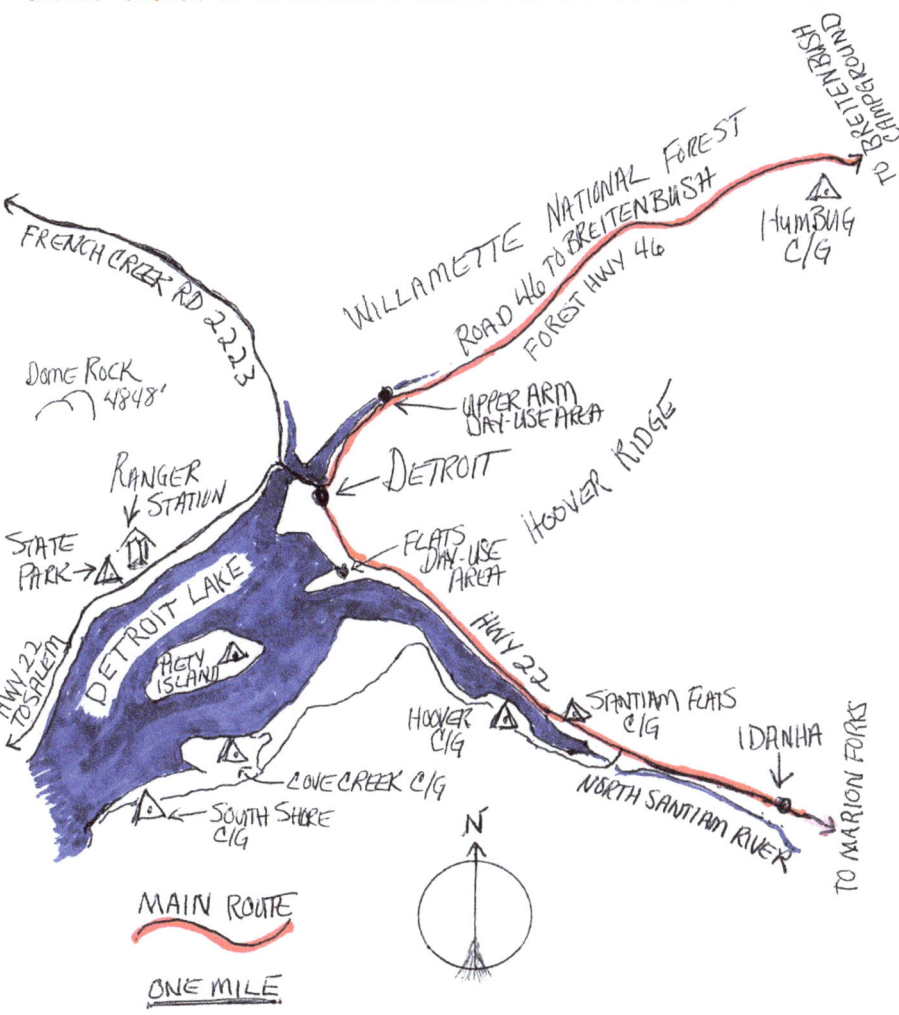

The Whitewater Road is heavily traveled during the hiking season because it's the easiest way to access the popular hiking trail to the **Jefferson Park** area north of Mount Jefferson. The road starts out with some car-eating potholes as it follows Whitewater Creek uphill. It's about seven miles from the highway to the trailhead parking area, elevation 4,120 feet. The trail meets the PCT about 3.5 miles from the parking lot.

Studded with alpine lakes and mind-blowing views of glacier-carved Mount Jefferson, Jefferson Park is usually crawling with day hikers and PCT hikers during the late summer and early fall season. The

Forest Service has restricted camping in the basin with most sites well away from water's edge. Get off the trail to find more secluded and private tent sites.

Back on Highway 22 heading north from the Whitewater Road intersection, the next point of interest on the North Santiam River is Whispering Falls Campground.

WHISPERING FALLS CAMPGROUND: Elevation 2,000 feet.

The campground has 16 sites laid out in a loop with water and vault toilets. The "Whispering Falls" can be viewed across the river from site number eight. The falls are formed by Misery Creek as it joins the North Santiam.

Idanha: (Pronounced: *eye-DAN'-uh*) Not much going on in Idanha these days — the town was at its peak during the heyday of railroad construction in the late 1880s. The town boomed again during construction of the dam forming Detroit Lake in the late 1940s. Today the town has a population of about 130 souls. A small grocery store and cafe survive, but not much else is left from the brief heyday of railroad construction. As we leave Idanha it's just a short drive to Detroit Lake.

DETROIT LAKE TO OLALLIE LAKE

Our next big stop is Detroit, the commercial center of the upper Santiam Valley, but don't expect to take delivery on a shiny new Ford or Chevy. A shiny new rainbow trout or kokanee would be more in the realm of possibility.

Detroit Lake Area: The settlement was originally named Coe and was essentially a logging and railroad town before the post-World War II construction of the dam. The name was officially changed to Detroit when a post office was established here in 1891 at the behest of a fair number of Michiganders living in the area at that time. For many years the only access to Detroit was via the railroad until a road was opened in 1926. The rail line, the **Oregon Pacific Railroad**, was being constructed through here to cross the Cascades at Santiam Pass, but was never completed beyond Idanha. Later, some tracks were laid near Santiam Pass (originally called Hogg Pass) and Hogg Rock so the company could claim rail service across the Cascade Summit.

The colorful character behind the railroad was **Thomas Egeton Hogg**. Born in Baltimore in 1828, Mr. Hogg later pirated a Union ship in Mexico during the American Civil War. Captured and

Region 7 — Santiam Pass to Olallie Lake

Eclectic sculptures grace the streets of downtown Detroit.

convicted, Hogg spent time in Alcatraz and San Quentin Prisons before being released. Records show he moved to Corvallis, Oregon in 1871 and added "Colonel" to his name even though he had no rank in the Confederate Navy or Army. Teaming up with Oregon banker Wallis Nash to promote the railroad, Hogg raised millions of dollars for the newly incorporated Oregon Pacific Railroad. The first leg of the railroad was completed from Corvallis to Yaquina Bay on the Pacific Coast in 1885, and a grand depot was constructed in Corvallis in 1887. Pushing the railroad eastward up the Santiam River was plagued by bad weather and fiscal mismanagement. By 1891 the railroad was bankrupt, and Colonel Hogg moved back east where he died in 1898.

On April 1st, 1949 workers began the construction of the dam that would form Detroit Lake. The town boomed during dam construction with over 3,000 workers on the job. Because the original town site was being flooded by the newly formed Detroit Lake, many of the buildings and businesses relocated to where the town is today, near the confluence of the North Santiam and Breitenbush Rivers. A high school and elementary school were built, along with a hotel, a church, a couple of taverns, and even a movie theater — the Canyon Theater 1947–1952.

Northern Oregon Backroads Guide to the PCT

The bridge crosses the Breitenbush River, marking the point where it enters Detroit Lake.

Quieter times prevail now. The town doesn't present itself as much from the highway: a motel or two, a couple of restaurants, grocery stores, and a gas station. The quiet and shady residential area is tucked away between the highway and the lake. The official year-round census is around 200 people, but many out-of-towners own homes here that are seasonally occupied — look out for the giant speed-bumps in front of the fancy summer houses.

KC's Cafe is tucked away along the south part of Detroit's commercial district. Look for the brightly painted purple building with the outdoor deck surrounded by a purple fence. With lattes and breakfast served all day and great cheeseburgers to boot, KC's also serves ice cream. Scarf your cheeseburger and milkshake at the "Map Table," where the Detroit Ranger District Map is stretched out beneath a sheet of glass in the dining room.

The Cedars Restaurant and Bar offers a great Bloody Mary that probably contains a good portion of your recommended daily vitamins and fiber. The bar is a testament to the region's logging history with giant antique chainsaws suspended from the ceiling and logging paraphernalia scattered about the barroom.

Region 7 — Santiam Pass to Olallie Lake

The two groceries in town are well stocked and offer fishing tackle along with deli items ranging from pizza slices to salads and specialty coffee drinks. Two marinas in the town area offer moorage (when the lake is full) and full service bars and cafes. A great website for local events, lodging and more is found at detroitlakeoregon.org.

The **Detroit Ranger Station** is located west of town on Highway 22. The ranger station is a good source for local trail information in the Mount Jefferson Wilderness Area and has maps of the region. The **Detroit Ranger District Map** is detailed and shows all the trailheads for the west side of Mount Jeff, plus campgrounds and trails in the Detroit neighborhood.

Forest Road 46 / Breitenbush River: As we leave Detroit Lake via Road 46 we encounter the **Upper Arm Day-Use Area** on our left. This is a popular place to bank fish with a wheelchair accessible pier when the lake is full. Riverside picnic tables are available and short paths connect the fishing pier with the parking area. The park marks the head of navigation for most boaters as the **Breitenbush River meets Detroit Reservoir**.

"Gotta stick?" Look for turn-outs along the Breitenbush River to enjoy the sparkling waters.

Northern Oregon Backroads Guide to the PCT

The 46 Road continues upriver in a northeasterly direction. Several informal campsites are along the road as we climb steadily up the river valley. The first Forest Service Campground we encounter along the way is Humbug Campground.

Humbug Campground: The campground is laid out in a double loop among the trees above the Breitenbush River. None of the campsites are waterfront but are connected to the river by trails. Each site has a table and fire ring. A couple of the sites can accommodate trailers to 25 feet. The campground has vault toilets and water.

Breitenbush Hot Springs: Advertising itself as an "Intentional Community" (not an accident I guess!), the hot springs operation covers 154 acres and features seven major geothermal springs. The owners are also the operators and exist, to one extent or another, as members of the commune. There is no tolerance for drugs, alcohol, cell phones, or dogs among the retreat's guests. Anyone not following the rules is asked to leave immediately. Guests are served vegetarian fare in the mess hall, prepared by one of various members of the community.

Breitenbush Hot Springs
503-854-3320

The 4220 Road to Breitenbush Lake — sometimes it's hard to tell where the rocks end and the road begins.

Region 7 — Santiam Pass to Olallie Lake

MAP R7.4: BREITENBUSH LAKE & BEYOND TO OLALLIE LAKE

Expect a bit of an authoritarian atmosphere to this little Utopia; keeping everyone in line must be a full-time task. Don't show up here unannounced; you will be told to leave immediately.

The assorted buildings associated with the community are spread haphazardly about the property and are constantly being repaired, remodeled, or updated.

Clothing is optional in the pools and on the grounds so this probably isn't the place for shy or modest individuals.

Breitenbush Campground: This campground is on the Breitenbush River with several near-riverfront sites. Big trees and the sound of water are the sensory experiences here. Accessible vault toilets and 22 sites accommodating trailers to 35 feet await the camper.

BREITENBUSH LAKE ROAD / 4220 ROAD INTERSECTION:
Elevation 3,570 feet

⇨ **Note: The 4220 Road is not suitable for passenger cars.**

The road to **Breitenbush Lake** starts out wide and easy; climbing slightly uphill, the good gravel road lures the unwary to continue. A big, heavy-duty gate is at the one-mile mark; this is a good place to turn around if you're not ready for the challenges of the 4220 Road.

The road begins to deteriorate as we head uphill from the gate. Brushy in places with ruts, meeting traffic heading downhill becomes a concern. The road is slow (allow about 40 minutes from the gate to the lake), but there are spots along the way where turn-offs are possible. About five miles from the mondo gate, and after climbing a long and rocky grade, the road reaches a saddle and we come to a **junction with the Pacific Crest Trail, elevation 5,508 feet**. The parking area is large and can accommodate a trailer turn-around for those who are brave enough (or foolish enough) to haul a trailer up here.

Breitenbush Lake is the headwater of the North Fork Breitenbush River and is officially on **Warm Springs Reservation** land. The tribal council allows public use of the lake; please treat this resource with respect. The campground is nicely situated on the west side of the lake with tables and fire rings. The road to the lake limits big motor homes and trailers; the camp is best suited for car and tent campers. The lake is fairly shallow but covers several acres. A path leads around the south side to an old shelter.

Region 7 — Santiam Pass to Olallie Lake

Along the pathway, the trail crosses a small wooden footbridge spanning the North Fork Breitenbush River. There's no potable water at the campground but a flow of water from a plastic pipe issues forth next to the footbridge. This water is not tested for drinking quality but I can personally attest to its cold, invigorating qualities on a hot day.

The lake's waters brim over a shallow rip-rap and flow west along a braided course through a meadow before gathering steam and coursing down the mountain, joining forces with other Breitenbush waters flowing west from Mount Jefferson into Detroit Lake.

On the 4220 Road Heading North: After leaving Breitenbush Lake the 4220 Road begins to climb. The road is extremely rough and rocky. Most "normal" weather years, this stretch of the Skyline Road is closed by snow until late June or early July. The road heads northeast, and we pass another shallow lake on our right before the road turns north and crosses a divide. The road touches the shore of **Spoon Lake** (elevation 5,638 feet) a short way past the divide. There's room to camp here next to the road. A secondary road heads east from here climbing to a quarry and a turnaround with more views of Olallie Basin to our north and Mount Jefferson to the south.

Leaving Spoon Lake behind, the road switch-backs downhill as we bounce our way to beautiful Horseshoe Lake and Horseshoe Lake Campground.

Horseshoe Lake: Elevation 5,345 feet.

Horseshoe is about the most isolated of the major lakes along the 4220 Road; it's miles of rough road to get here any way you go. The pay-off is a gorgeous, quiet spot among the big timber. Pleasant campsites are located at **Horseshoe Lake Campground** and the lake offers paddlers a chance to explore the peaceful shores of the "U" shaped lake. Fishing can be good early in the season before the waters get too warm. The lake covers 14 to 15 acres and harbors both brook and rainbow trout. It's possible to fish this lake from shore but a floating craft offers the angler more opportunities.

Hikers can hook-up with the PCT by walking about a mile west along the **712 Trail**. The trailhead is on the north side of Horseshoe Lake. After leaving Horseshoe Lake, the 4220 Road continues very rough as it heads downhill to our next stop at Monon Lake.

Monon Lake: Monon Lake is the second largest lake in the area (after Olallie Lake) and covers more than 94 acres. This lake, like all of the myriad marshes, ponds, and lakes of the **14,238-acre Olallie Lakes Scenic Area**, was scooped out by glaciers. There is very little inflow to Monon and Olallie Lakes since they are located near the top of the Clackamas drainage. There's enough annual snow melt and rainfall (in non-drought years) to keep the water levels near constant.

The lake is stocked with rainbow trout and an occasional brook trout is hooked here. A small boat launch is at the northwest end of the lake; no motors allowed. Although Monon is mostly shallow, deep pockets of water are on the northeast arm of the lake. A few informal campsite possibilities are at Monon but better camping lies just ahead at Olallie Lake and the beginning of Region Eight.

END OF REGION SEVEN

Region Eight begins at Olallie Lake and follows the Skyline Road north. After exploring the northern part of the Olallie Lakes Scenic Area, we'll hook-up with the 110 Road and explore a piece of Oregon's remaining old growth forest. Further north lies Timothy Lake, Frog Lake, Barlow Pass, Trillium Lake, Mount Hood, and the end of Region Eight at Government Camp.

A trail circles Region Eight's Trillium Lake, offering views of snow-clad Mount Hood.

MULTI-REGION MAP 2: REGIONS 8 & 9

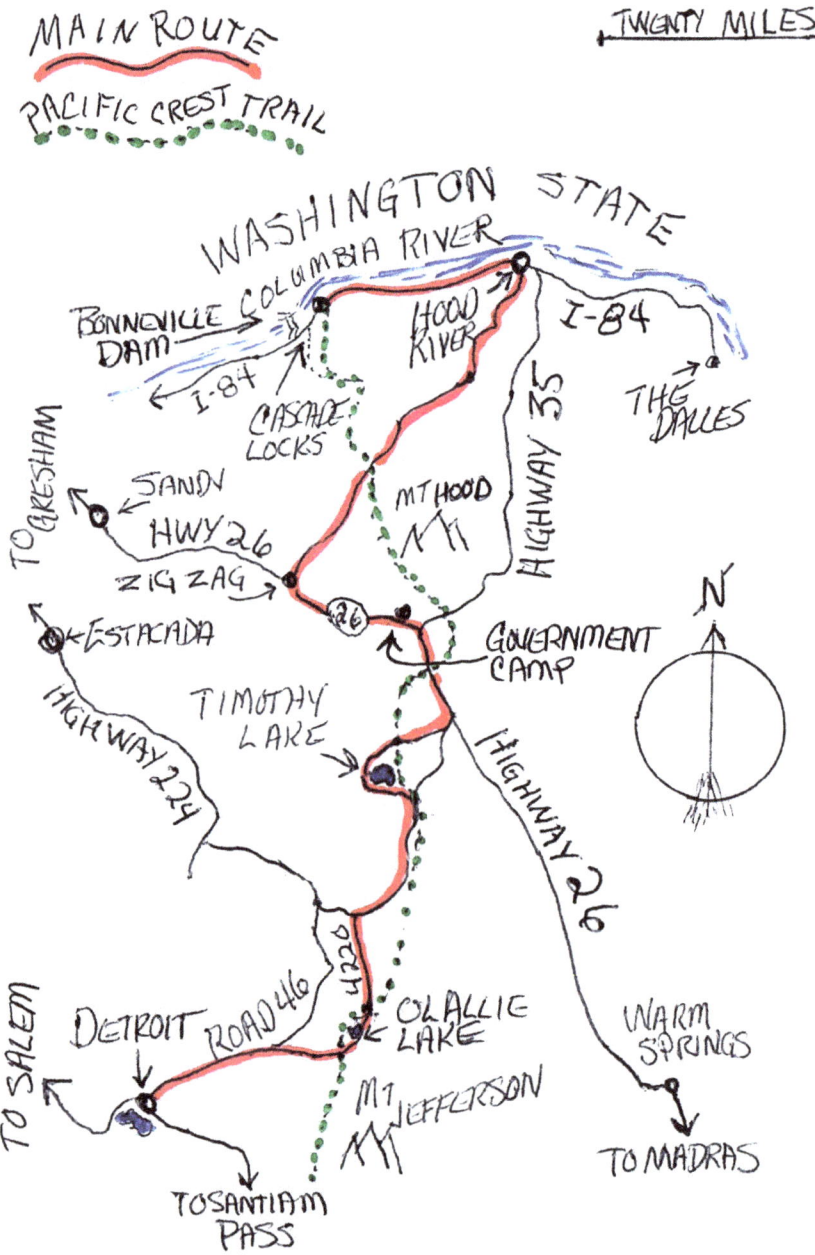

REGION EIGHT
Olallie Lake to Government Camp

The road to Timberline Lodge — Mount Hood lies near the end of Region Eight.

It doesn't matter where you came from. All that matters is where you're going....
—*Bob Marley*

Region 8 — Olallie Lake to Government Camp

ROUTE DESCRIPTION

Beginning from Olallie Lake Resort, the Main Route heads north on the sometimes rough 4220 / Oregon Skyline Road to its intersection with the unpaved 110 Road. We stay on the 110 Road to our next turn onto the paved 42 Road.

The 42 Road takes us north past Clackamas Lake to our turn onto the paved 57 Road at Timothy Lake. After exploring the south part of Timothy Lake the route crosses the Timothy Lake Dam. After crossing the dam, we'll turn north on the improved gravel 5890 Road, explore the north arm of Timothy Lake, cross the PCT and arrive at the paved 58 Road and the option to take a gander at interesting Little Crater Lake.

From the intersection with the 58 Road we'll skirt Clear Lake along its southern side. After meeting State Route 26, we'll head north to our next crossing of the PCT at Wapanitia Pass (Frog Lake). State Route 26 heads north to optional explorations of Barlow Pass (another crossing of the PCT) and the old Barlow Toll Road route along the White River and Mount Hood's Timberline Lodge. Region Eight ends at the town of Government Camp.

ROAD CONDITIONS

⇨ **Note:** *All of the roads along the Main Route are suitable for passenger cars (in good weather) with reasonable clearance.*

The 4220 Road to and from Olallie Lake Resort is rough with serious potholes but can be navigated by passenger cars with caution in good weather. The continuation of the 4220 Road north of its intersection with the 4690 Road is rough for 1.7 miles before it becomes paved with some sneaker potholes.

The 110 Road has a sign at its beginning warning that it's not maintained for passenger vehicles. Nothing technically difficult about the 110 Road though, so it's your call on whether or not you want to drive the family sedan on this road. Map R8.3 shows the optional way. There are no other road issues along the remainder of Region Eight in good weather.

⇦ *The high country of The Olallie Lakes Scenic Area holds more than 100 lakes.*

RECOMMENDED MAPS FOR REGION EIGHT
The following maps are useful supplements to this guidebook.
- *Mount Hood National Forest Map*
- Benchmark Maps – *Oregon Road and Recreation Atlas*, pages 49 and 50

The Mount Hood National Forest Map is available at ranger stations and on-line at http://www.fs.usda.gov/mthood . Benchmark maps are available at book stores, sporting goods stores, and online at benchmarkmaps.com.

OPTIONAL ROADS IN REGION EIGHT
Vehicles with reasonable clearance should have no issues with clearance or traction in good weather. Optional side trips to Summit Lake, Little Crater Lake, Barlow Pass, Timberline Lodge, and Trillium Lake are included in the descriptions.

PCT ACCESS POINTS
You can access the PCT at six points in Region Eight.
1. The Pacific Crest Trail crosses the 4220 Road near Olallie Lake Resort and parallels the road north to Olallie Meadow. From here to Joe Graham Horsecamp, it's 30 trail miles.
2. The PCT next crosses at Joe Graham Horse Camp near the intersection of Forest Highways 42 and 57, south of Timothy Lake.

Look for colorful shooting stars near Olallie Meadow Campground.

Region 8 — Olallie Lake to Government Camp

3. The PCT crosses the 5890 Road north of Timothy Lake.

4. The Pacific Crest Trail crosses Oregon Highway 26 at Wapanitia Pass and the Frog Lake trailhead. It's 14 trail miles from Joe Graham.

5. Our next meeting with the PCT is at Barlow Pass on Oregon Highway 35. It's 5 trail miles from Frog Lake.

6. The PCT is accessible by a short connector trail from Timberline Lodge. The Lodge is 5 trail miles from Barlow Pass.

MAIN ROADS IN ORDER OF TRAVEL

Forest Road 4220	Also called the Skyline Road, we'll head north from Olallie Lake Resort.
Forest Road 110	This drive through an old forest is basically an extension of the Skyline Road.
Forest Road 4240	We're on this road for about 0.5 miles to our turn onto Forest Highway 42.
Forest Highway 42	We'll stay on this paved road to our next turn onto Forest Highway 57.
Forest Highway 57	This paved road leads us to an exploration of south Timothy Lake.
Forest Road 5890	After crossing Timothy Lake Dam, we'll turn north onto the 5890 Road. Paved at first, it turns to improved gravel before crossing the PCT.
Forest Highway 58	We are on this road for a few hundred feet before turning left onto the 2660 Road.
Forest Road 2660	We are on this gravel road for 0.8 miles before turning east onto the 4290 Road.
Forest Road 4290	This paved road takes us to a stop sign at the 42 Road.
Forest Highway 42	We're back on the 42 Road for about a mile to a stop sign on State Highway 26.
State Highway 26	We'll stay on the State Highway to Government Camp and the end of Region Eight.

Northern Oregon Backroads Guide to the PCT

ROAD NOTES – REGION EIGHT

We begin our explorations at Olallie Lake tand then head to the 110 road intersection. A variety of large and small lakes offer many scenic and camping options in this section of our route.

Olallie Lake Area: Olallie Lake (pronounced o-LAW-lee), surface elevation 4,950 feet, is the namesake lake of the **Olallie Lakes Scenic Area**. Looking at a map of this area should make a lover of mountain lakes drool... Well over 100 lakes of varying size are scattered about the general area, including several on Warm Springs Reservation land. Olallie is the largest lake, spanning about a mile end to end, and covering more than 185 acres.

Three campgrounds and a day-use area are located on the lake, along with Olallie Lake Resort. Many hiking trails are nearby, with the trail circling Olallie being a popular day-hike. Other trails lead east to lakes on reservation land that are open to the public with a tribal permit (contact the Confederated Tribes of Warm Springs at 541-553-1161 for info). The PCT crosses the 4220 Road adjacent to the resort and the Forest Service Guard Station on Olallie's north shore. A day-use area on the north shore has a boat ramp, and there's a boat ramp at Peninsula Campground; no motors allowed.

The day-use area at Olallie Lake has a boat launch.

Region 8 — Olallie Lake to Government Camp

Peninsula Campground has a pleasant fishing pier with views of Mount Jefferson when the fish aren't biting.

Fishing for rainbow trout is popular during the summer months. The roads into Olallie are typically snowed-in until early June (when the fishing is best) in most years with normal snow fall. Trollers use small lures and spinner-bait combinations to catch fish here. The fish average about 11–14 inches long, and an occasional brook trout may be in the mix. Fly fishermen work the near-shore areas in the evenings and early mornings.

CAMPGROUNDS ON OLALLIE LAKE

Peninsula Campground: As advertised, Peninsula is situated on a tongue of land extending into the lake's southwest side. Laid out in a loop, this largest of all Olallie Lake camps features 35 fee sites with a few walk-in only. A beautiful fishing pier with a spectacular view of Mount Jefferson will keep you happy if the fish aren't biting.

Camp Ten: Located on the west side of Olallie Lake, this campground has 10 fee sites, vault toilets, and no water. There's a place to slip a small paddle craft into the water, but use the nearby Peninsula boat launch for bigger boats.

Paul Dennis Campground: This campground features 12 drive-in sites, 3 walk-in sites, and two oversize yurts. The yurts have two bedrooms and can sleep up to 6 people each. There's no electricity or running water in either unit, but kerosene lights are provided. Managed by Olallie Lake Resort, reservations can be booked via the resort's website. Potable water is available at the resort. Paul Dennis is situated on the northeast side of the lake past the resort.

OLALLIE LAKE RESORT

This resort suffers from a bit of a personality conflict. The owner values the isolation of the resort and the peaceful vibe of the wild country. Yet, the need to make money forces them to allow the public to rent cabins and boats here. The owner doesn't post a phone number so the only way to rent a cabin is via the Internet.

Olallie Lake Resort
olallielakeresort.com

Many visitors want to pull up the drawbridge once they've discovered this near-wilderness gem; road signs pointing the way here are regularly vandalized, destroyed, or removed. The resort was built in 1933, and little has changed since then. There's no electricity at the cabins, no phones (your cell phone won't work here), and wood stoves provide heat. The tiny store offers little more than camper's supplies, hot coffee, and a registry for hikers on the Pacific Crest Trail. Bring all of your housekeeping supplies with you when you rent a cabin here; it's a long drive to the nearest store.

Olallie Lake Resort rents rowboats and paddle craft.

Region 8 — Olallie Lake to Government Camp

Deep and cold, Head Lake lies just across the road from Olallie Lake.

Everyone is asked not to swim in Olallie Lake; it's used as the domestic water supply for the resort. Well-behaved dogs are allowed at the resort but be forewarned you'll probably get yelled at by someone if they see your dog swimming in the lake. Those wanting to swim are encouraged to visit nearby Head Lake. This little lake is deep and a short walk across the 4220 Road from the resort. A small parking area is here for the Pacific Crest Trail as well.

Gazing south from the rowboat marina, the awesome presence of Mount Jefferson, Oregon's second highest mountain, reigns over the scene. **Olallie Butte, elevation 7,216 feet**, brackets the horizon to the east. Big views of the mountains and the surrounding country lure hikers and fishermen to explore this lake-strewn landscape. Mosquitoes can be a problem early in the summer season so come prepared if you're camping or hiking. The latter part of June and early July brings wildflowers and an interesting event with the mating season for **nighthawks** (*Chordeiles minor*). These graceful fliers engage in steep nosedives from high in the sky, vibrating their primary wing feathers as they abruptly pull up, which creates an odd humming sound impressive to other nighthawks, no doubt. Late August and early September brings more consistent weather with fewer bugs and people.

Northern Oregon Backroads Guide to the PCT

MAP R8.1: OLALLIE LAKE TO THE 110 ROAD

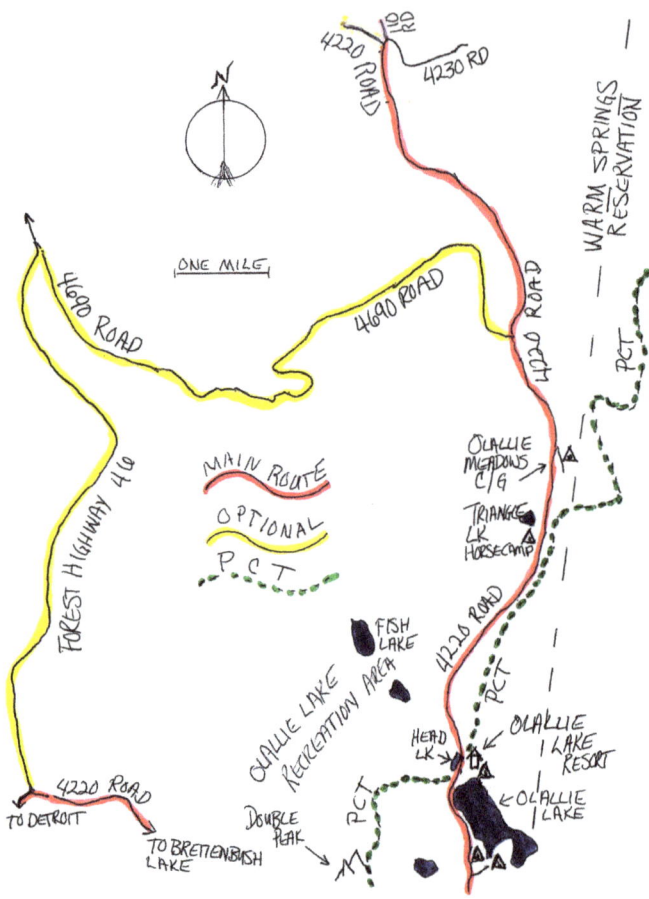

The Olallie Guard Station cabin is available for rent early July to September. The cabin is at the entrance to the resort and just across the 4220 Road from the PCT at Head Lake. Check the web for available dates.

Heading North on the Skyline Road: After leaving Olallie Lake Resort, the 4220 / Skyline Road becomes incrementally better — just the usual unavoidable potholes and minor washes to contend with. Immediately after the resort road we come to Head Lake on our left. Find an informal campsite here and a place to slide a small boat into the tiny body of water.

Lower Lake Campground: The road crosses a small creek via a metal slat bridge before coming to the entrance to Lower Lake

Region 8 — Olallie Lake to Government Camp

The picturesque old cabin at Olallie Meadow is well preserved.

Campground, elevation 4,825 feet. The 8 campsites connect to Lower Lake by way of the 717 Trail. The trail to Lower Lake is mostly downhill and pretty easy going. Once the trail hits the 14-acre lake, it continues along the shoreline northward to some good hike-in campsites. The 717 Trail continues northwest a little more than a half-mile from Lower Lake. After a steep pitch downhill, the path arrives at big, deep **Fish Lake, elevation 4,298 feet**. Both of these lakes are among the best fishing lakes in the Scenic Area with Lower Lake being a good rainbow fishery and 20-acre Fish Lake being productive for smaller but abundant cutthroat and brook trout.

Triangle Lake: After leaving the Lower Lake Campground, the 4220 Road heads northeast paralleling the PCT as we cross beneath a set of high tension power lines. A short way past the power lines, we arrive at the entrance to **Triangle Lake Equestrian Campground**, elevation 4,600 feet. This is actually the backdoor to the campground and the road is not signed here. The campground road heads north and connects up with the 4220 Road in a few blocks. The campground is not situated on Triangle Lake but is connected by a very short (less than a city block) footpath, not open to horses. Another cluster of lakes lies just to the east with **Jude Lake** and **Russ Lake** being the largest.

Olallie Meadow Campground: Still heading north as we leave Triangle Lake behind, we bounce our way to Olallie Meadow Campground, elevation 4,495 feet. A spur road angles to our right as we pass the vault toilets and enter the campground. This is the first campground to go snow-free in the late spring to early summer. There are 7 sites here with a couple of spots big enough to maneuver a small trailer.

Olallie Meadow was once a large shallow lake but has filled with sediment to form the soggy meadows here today. A cabin on the west side of the meadow is open to the public. Rather dark and spooky on the inside, the outside of the cabin has a small covered porch and a picnic table. A trailhead at the end of the campground road leads to tiny Brook Lake and beyond to Jude and Russ Lakes.

MAP R8.2: THE 110 ROAD TO SUMMIT LAKE

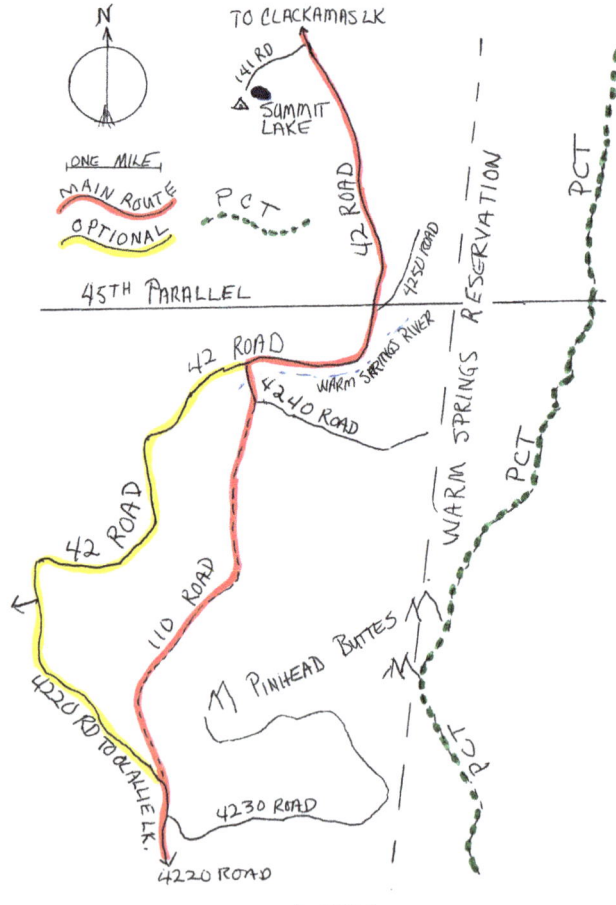

Region 8 — Olallie Lake to Government Camp

We leave the entrance to Olallie Meadow Campground and continue north on the Skyline Road. An informational sign on the left describes the area we've just driven. A little more than a mile past the sign brings us to the signed intersection with the 4690 Road. The sign pointing the way to Olallie Lake is constantly being vandalized — keeps folks guessing, I suppose.

Skyline Road / 4690 Road Intersection: The 4690 Road is the improved route back to civilization, and after a couple miles of gravel, it is paved to its intersection with Forest Highway 46. Those of you who followed the optional route, described in Region Seven for avoiding the very rough beginning of The Skyline / 4220 Road to Breitenbush Lake, came in this way.

The Main Route continues north from the Olallie Lake sign, staying on the Skyline / 4220 Road. That's right, not the wide and inviting gravel road heading west, it's the road heading north that's strewn with logs and debris that we want. If you've already driven the length of the Skyline Road from Breitenbush Lake to this point, you'll chuckle when I say this road is on the rough side.

The worst part of the road ahead is the first half-mile or so; not saying you won't encounter some rough spots but I've driven a passenger car through here with no problem. It's about 1.7 miles of rough road and just when you are about to curse the writer of this book and your decision to follow its advice, the 4220 / Skyline Road becomes paved. We'll stay on this luxury thoroughfare for a little over 2 miles before we reach a three-way intersection with Forest Road 110 dead ahead and the 4230 Road going right (east).

FOREST ROAD 110 TO TIMOTHY LAKE

This segment takes us on a drive through an old forest and an exploration of Clackamas Lake before delivering us to Timothy Lake.

FOREST ROAD 110: Elevation 4,279 feet.

The picture sign at the beginning of the 110 Road illustrates the outline of a passenger car, shot full of holes, with the words "Not Maintained" above and below. Don't let that scare you away though. In dry weather this road is doable in just about any vehicle (if it's not shot full of holes). Is this road worth taking? I would say yes, but remember I said in dry weather... **if you have doubts, follow the optional road on Map R8.2**.

Northern Oregon Backroads Guide to the PCT

Chainsaw-wielding motorists clear the way along the 110 Road.

The road passes by a couple of old clear-cuts, but by and large, the 110 Road is one of the nicest forest roads I've driven and takes the driver through miles of old growth forests with plenty of opportunities to see wildlife and wildflowers. This forest road is essentially an extension of the 4220 / Skyline Road and contours along the west side of the oddly named West Pinhead Butte. The 110 Road takes about 30 to 40 minutes to drive if you don't stop and gawk.

After leaving the pavement, the big trees line the way until we come to a logged area uphill where trees have toppled, blocking the road. Chainsaw-wielding drivers have cleared the logs through here with a couple of tight squeezes along the way. After leaving the clear-cut, the old trees shelter an understory of shade-loving plants. Look for flickers and woodpeckers, who thrive in this old forest environment.

On hot summer days the forest of big Douglas firs and hemlocks can feel several degrees cooler. The moss-draped trees provide a backdrop to towering rhododendrons that can put on quite a show during their brief flowering season. The road provides a few challenges for the driver; some spots can be muddy during the wet season, and there's

Region 8 — Olallie Lake to Government Camp

always the chance of a fallen tree blocking your path.

The only road that intersects the 110 Road is the once gated 120 Road. This road more closely follows the PCT and looks tempting on the map but I don't recommend taking it. Someone has removed the gates on both ends of this road but because the road was gated for years, it's extremely brushy and washed in a couple of places.

Beyond the 120 Road intersection, the 110 Road continues northward going downhill through more beautiful big timber before flattening out and passing by some potential campsites. The road then delivers us to a three-way intersection with the 4240 Road where we stay left, heading downhill on the 4240 Road before crossing the headwaters of the Warm Springs River and coming to a stop sign marking Forest Highway 42.

> ⇨ **Note:** *On the east side of the bridge marking the Warm Springs River, a short secondary road heads north and along the banks of the river (at this point Warm Springs River is a creek). Most maps mark this spot as the site of Warm Springs Cabin and a mining claim.*

I've looked around the area a couple of times, searching for the cabin site, and have come up with nothing more than an ancient

Hounds tongue sports bright blue flowers and is often found in streamside meadows.

outhouse and some interesting bog-loving plants. There are a couple of potential campsites here, but its kind of close to the Forest Highway. The mining claim is for an open pit (gravel?) operation just to the south.

FOREST HIGHWAY 42 HEADING NORTH: Elevation, 3,726 ft.

⇨ **Special note:** *Geography Nerds alert!*

After leaving the 4240 Road intersection, Forest Highway 42 heads east before turning sharply north; first intersecting the 4245 Road to the right and then the 4250 Road, also to the right. A few yards past the 4250 Road intersection we will cross the **45th parallel**, exactly half way between the North Pole and Earth's equator. Green Bay Wisconsin in the United States and Milan, Italy both lie just north of the 45th parallel for reference. Legend tells us that a boiled egg will stand on its end at this point (I'm kidding, right?). I left my egg shell there...can you see other people's dedications to this imaginary line?

After we pass the half-way point between freezing ass cold and too damned hot, the 42 Highway heads uphill. As we near the top of the hill we'll see the turn-off (comes up quickly) to the left (west) to Summit Lake. Both Clackamas and Wasco Counties divide at this intersection, elevation 4,180 feet.

SUMMIT LAKE: Surface elevation, 4,215 feet.

It's a steep turn up the paved part of the 141 Road before leveling off and becoming improved gravel. Drive about a mile to the campground with restricted driving access near the lake. With a small spot to launch a boat and a turn-around, there are 5 fee sites and a couple of them are short walk-ins. This lake is near the actual summit (hence the name perhaps?) of the Clackamas drainage with the Oak Grove Fork Clackamas lying to our north and the main stem of the Clackamas River draining the country to our south.

Back on the 42 Road Heading North: After leaving the Summit Lake Road, Forest Highway 42 heads downhill in earnest. Breaks in the trees along our way to Clackamas Lake show our first glimpse of Mount Hood, many miles to the north. From the Summit Lake turn-off its about four miles to the Clackamas Lake Campground and Guard Station.

CLACKAMAS LAKE CAMPGROUND & TRAILHEAD:

The campground is laid out in a loop and contains a total of 46

Region 8 — Olallie Lake to Government Camp

campsites. Many of the campsites are for horse campers with gated corrals and loading ramps. There are accessible vault toilets and pump-handle water.

Shallow Clackamas Lake, near the head water of the Oak Grove Fork Clackamas River, is a short hike from the eastern edge of the campground. The trailhead was once the site of a private cabin now converted to a public day-use area. The trail to the lake is less than a quarter-mile long and crosses a sensitive marsh area. Hikers walk across a boardwalk to a small wooden deck on the shore of Clackamas Lake. Bring your folding chair and binoculars to observe red-wing blackbirds and other marsh-loving birds. Look for marsh-loving plants and butterflies along the way.

After leaving the campground, we'll continue north on Forest Highway 42. In a very short distance we arrive at the Clackamas Lake Ranger Station.

Clackamas Lake Ranger Station Historic District: The first building here was constructed by the district's first ranger, Joe Graham, in 1906. Covering about 4 acres, the area has several old buildings of historic significance. The old district office is now a museum open to the public during the summer months. A total of 11 buildings date back to the 1930s and the hey-day of the Civilian

The boardwalk to Clackamas Lake ends at a small landing.

Northern Oregon Backroads Guide to the PCT

Conservation Corps.

Constructed and decorated in "Forest Service" style, the rustic wooden structures served as residences and barracks for forest fire and work crews. Following World War II and the construction of modern roads to the area, there was less need to house overnight crews, and the buildings fell into disuse during the 1960s. The guard station was re-opened in 1972 and has remained in use since then. The ranger station compound was listed as an historic district in 1981.

Leaving the ranger station and continuing north on 42, we immediately cross the Oak Fork of the Clackamas River, flowing through a beautiful meadow.

INTERSECTION OF FOREST HIGHWAY 57: Elevation 3,350 ft.

This is a major intersection so take the time to stop and get your bearings before we proceed.

> ⇨ **Note:** *The Pacific Crest Trail follows the eastern shore of Timothy Lake. For those who wish to go that way, there are no road issues other than just plain boredom. The 4280 Road on Timothy's east side is improved gravel but offers little to the traveler with no lake access and no views.*

Turn left (west) on Forest Highway 57 to follow the Main Route to Timothy Lake. Or turn right (east) on 57 and arrive in short order at the entrance to Joe Graham Horse Camp. Just past the entrance to the camp is a parking area and marked trailhead for the **Pacific Crest Trail**, elevation 3,378 feet.

Joe Graham Horse Camp and the Pacific Crest Trail: The horse camp has 14 sites laid-out in a loop with pump-handle water, corrals, hitching posts, and vault toilets. There's easy access for horseback riders to the many trails in the area including the adjacent Pacific Crest Trail.

A sign marks the PCT trailhead near Joe Graham Horse Camp.

TIMOTHY LAKE TO GOVERNMENT CAMP

The final leg of Region Eight takes us on a tour of Timothy Lake then over Wapanitia Pass to the west side of the Cascades and beautiful, historic Timberline Lodge on Mount Hood.

TIMOTHY LAKE AREA

Timothy Lake, surface elevation at full pool 3,234 feet, is a hydro power reservoir formed by a dam on the Oak Grove Fork Clackamas River. The speed limit is 10 mph on the entire lake. Covering more than 1,400 acres, the waters of Timothy can be very productive for kokanee early in the season before the surface warms. Some brook trout to 5 pounds are caught here annually and rainbows are stocked in large quantities. Recreation is popular on the lake early in the summer when the reservoir is (usually) full. The four large, drive-in campgrounds on the south end of the lake can be packed on the Fourth of July and Memorial Day weekends. By late August, the reservoir has been drawn down and the waters have warmed. Large flats along the shoreline are exposed, and very few people use the lake after Labor Day.

The PCT traverses the lake's eastern shore. Map readers will notice that the route this book recommends passes along the lake's western shore. Drivers are, of course, free to follow the road more closely following the PCT along the eastern part of Timothy Lake (the 4280 Road), but I find little there to recommend to the sightseer.

The Main Route follows Forest Highway 57 along the south side of Timothy Lake, crosses the dam, then heads north on the 5820 Road. The four Forest Service Campgrounds arrayed along the south shore of Timothy Lake attract the majority of campers. Cove, also on the south shore, is a day-use area. Trail 528 circles Timothy Lake connecting all of the campgrounds and hooking up with the PCT along Timothy's eastern shore. It's about a 12-mile hike around the lake.

CAMPGROUNDS ON TIMOTHY LAKE

⇨ **Note:** *The south shore of Timothy is (virtually) one giant campground.*

Connected by a shoreline trail and the paved 57 Road, the four campgrounds and one day-use area listed below are on the south shore of Timothy Lake. Oak Fork is the easternmost of the bunch and connects via a short trail to the PCT. Meditation Point and North

Region 8 — Olallie Lake to Government Camp

MAP R8.3: TIMOTHY LAKE AREA

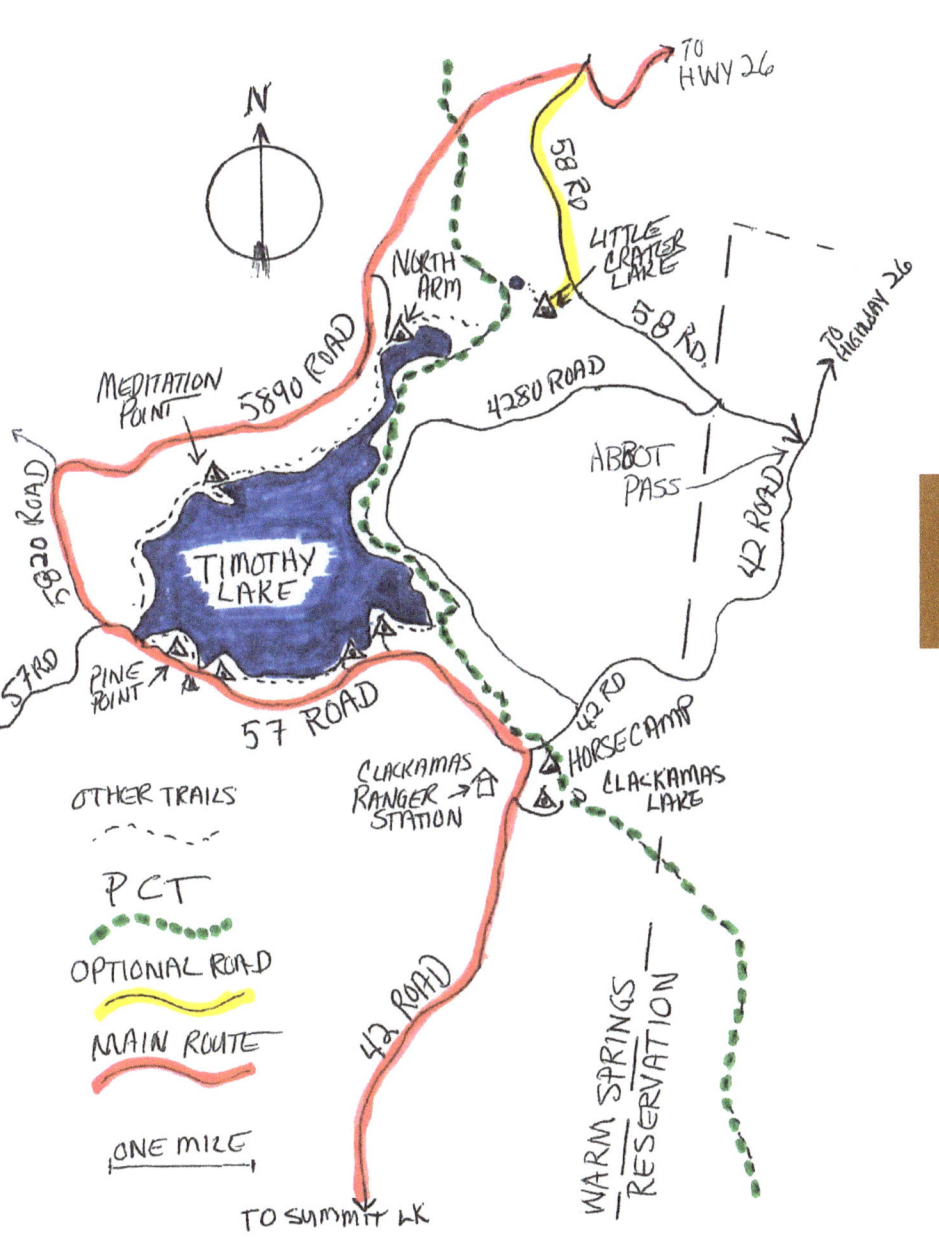

Arm Campgrounds are located along the north shore. For more information on area campgrounds look on-line at Portland General Electric's website pgeparks@pgn.com.

Oak Fork: The camp is located near where the Oak Fork Clackamas River spills into Timothy Lake. From the eastern edge of the campground, a trail connects with the PCT. The campground is above the lake and mostly situated in the big trees with trails connecting to the water. There are 47 sites, some large enough to accommodate trailers to 32 feet. A paved boat launch with a large parking area and day-use area is next to the lake.

Gone Creek: Gone Creek is the twin brother of Oak Fork Campground. With a large boat ramp, a nice day-use area, and 50 fee sites, Gone Creek stays busy when the lake is full.

Hoodview: They don't call it Hoodview for nothing. Several of the campsites are near the lake's shore and sport a great view of Mount Hood across the lake to the north. There's a large boat launch and day-use area (for registered campers only), along with 43 fee sites. The camp has water and accessible vault toilets.

Cove Day-Use Area: Cove used to be a walk-in campground with parking along the highway and was a quieter alternative to the big,

Little Crater Lake is actually an artesian spring on steroids.

Region 8 — Olallie Lake to Government Camp

drive-in campgrounds on the south side of Timothy Lake. Now it's day-use only here — no camping allowed.

Pine Point: This campground has 25 fee sites. Located on the eastern side of the dam, Pine Point's boat launch is the only one that's operational during low water. With a huge parking lot and giant day-use area, Pine Point is used extensively by day trippers from the Willamette Valley. A new group camp is being built across the 57 Road from Pine Point and is scheduled to be opened in 2016. From the Pine Point entrance, we continue west across the dam.

After crossing the Timothy Lake Dam, the Main Route heads north on the **5820 Road**. We leave Forest Highway 57 behind as we turn north on the paved 5820 Road. **We'll stay north on the 5820 Road for 1.2 miles to our turn at the 5890 Road.**

5890 Road Intersection: The Main Route heads north on the improved gravel 5890 road. From this intersection, it's 2.8 miles to the entrance of North Arm Campground. Along our way to North Arm Camp, we'll pass by the gated road/trail to Meditation Point. It's about 1.25 miles down to the camp along the road.

Meditation Point: Meditation Point is a boat-in campground along the northwest shore with 5 "official" sites. The campground, situated on a peninsula, can also be reached by trail.

North Arm Campground: North Arm Campground is the quietest of the drive-in campgrounds on Timothy Lake. Laid out in a linear form, North Arm Campground has been recently updated (2015) with additional campsites, bathrooms, and drinking water. The boat ramp and parking area have been enlarged, but the ramp is most usable during high water levels. When the water's low, much of the North Arm dries up.

> ⇨ **Note:** *The trail from the camp meets the PCT in about a half-mile.*

A trail leads from the north side of camp through beautiful meadows on the north side of the lake and meets up with the PCT. From the trail intersection, it's about a quarter-mile hike to Little Crater Lake.

Back on the 5890 Road Heading North: After leaving the North Arm Camp we continue north on the 5890 Road for 1.4 miles to a crossing of the **Pacific Crest Trail, elevation 3,367 feet**. One mile past the trailhead, we arrive at the paved Forest Highway 58.

Northern Oregon Backroads Guide to the PCT

INTERSECTION OF THE 5890 & 58 ROADS: Elevation 3,445 ft.

> ⇨ **Note:** *The optional side trip to Little Crater Lake begins here. It's 1.6 miles south of this intersection along Forest Highway 58 to the entrance to Little Crater Lake Campground and the trailhead (consult Map R8.4). It's well worth your time to explore enigmatic Little Crater Lake at less than a quarter-mile hike.*

The following intersections come up quickly, especially the first one! Be patient and use the maps you brought with you. (You did bring maps, right?) and follow the **Main Roads in Order of Travel** table at the beginning of Region Eight and you'll be fine.

After turning right (east) off the 5890 Road (and if you skip the side trip to Little Crater), **we're on Forest Highway 58 for a total of about 50 yards before we turn left (east) onto the 2660 Road**.

INTERSECTION OF FOREST HIGHWAY 58 & THE 2660 ROAD

After turning onto the paved 2660 Road, we will travel 0.8 miles to our next turn to the right (east) onto the 4290 Road.

> ⇨ **Note:** *The Pacific Crest Trail circles around Clear Lake to the north and the 2660 Road follows a sinuous course closer to the PCT than the roads I recommend. There's nothing wrong with taking the 2660 Road around Clear Lake other than the fact it offers no access to the PCT and no views.*

INTERSECTION OF THE 2660 & 4290 ROADS: After turning onto the 4290 Road, we'll drive 2.3 miles along the improved gravel road to a stop sign marking Forest Highway 42 where we'll turn left (east) onto 42.

INTERSECTION OF THE 4290 ROAD & FOREST HIGHWAY 42

We'll drive east about one mile on Forest Highway 42 to the stop sign marking Oregon Highway 26, where we'll turn left (north).

HEADING NORTH ON HIGHWAY 26: Join the rush of traffic on Highway 26 as we head north for about a mile and a half to the first turn on our left marking the road to **Clear Lake Campground**. Clear Lake (the Wasco County version) can be nice early in the year before the reservoir is drawn down. The campground offers 28 fee sites along with a boat launch. The camp can accommodate some large RVs, which can definitely be found here in the summer.

Back on Highway 26 heading north, the road climbs to the first of two passes along the crest country here. Blue Box Pass tops the

Region 8 — Olallie Lake to Government Camp

MAP R8.4: LITTLE CRATER & FROG LAKES AREA

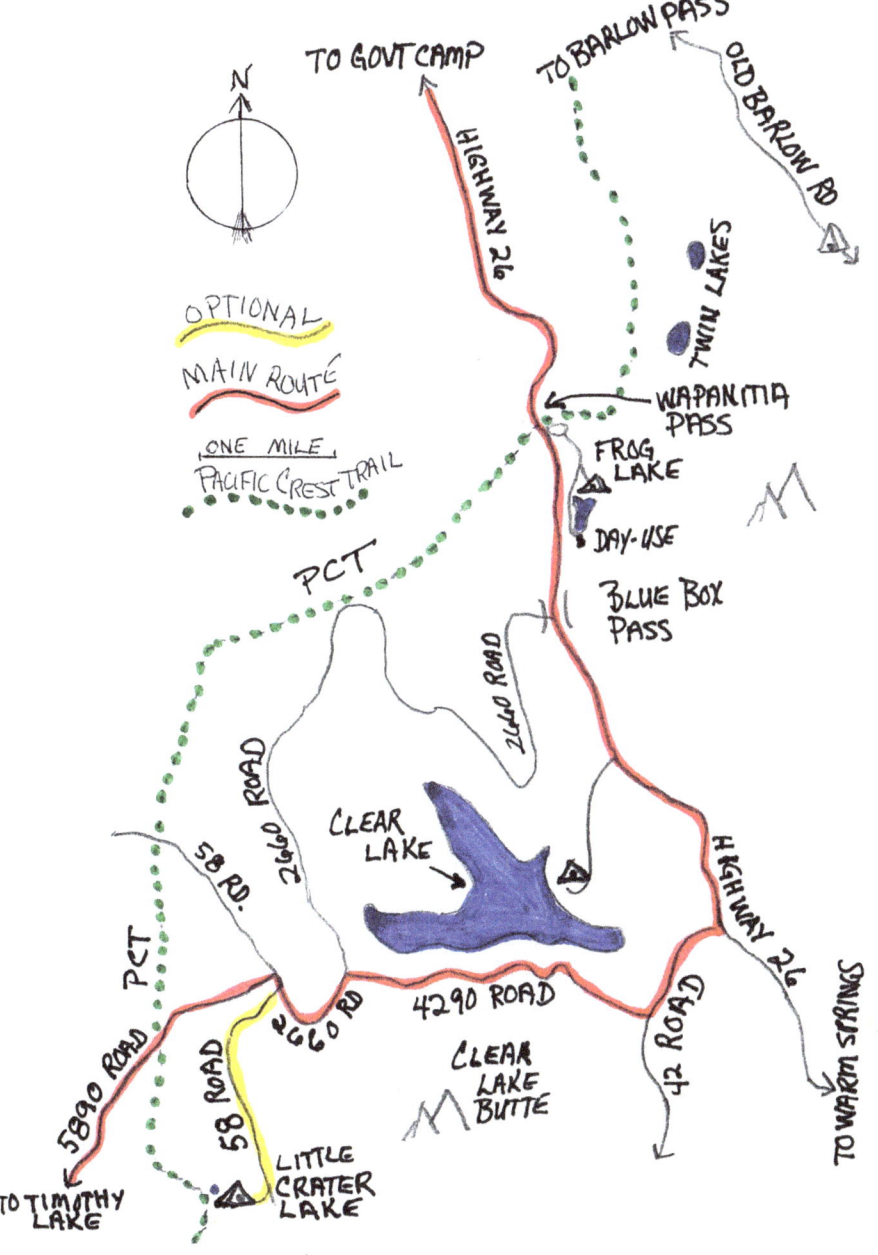

hill at 4,024 feet and Wapanitia Pass to our north summits at 3,952 feet. But before we get to Wapanitia Pass, we arrive at the **Frog Lake access to the Pacific Crest Trail**.

<u>FROG LAKE AREA:</u> Elevation 3,926 ft. at the PCT trailhead.

After pulling into the Frog Lake parking area for the PCT, the first thing you're going to notice is lots of asphalt. The powers that are have decided that this will be the mondo turn-around / parking lot of upper Highway 26. Good thing I guess; it's usually swarming with traffic in the summer. In the winter it's used by the snow-loving crowd and can be equally thronged. Hikers can also do day-hikes to the **Twin Lakes**, the first of which is about 2 miles from the trailhead.

Head south through the acres of asphalt and you'll quickly arrive at the entrance to Frog Lake Campground. The camp is popular and usually full on summer weekends. There are 33 fee sites, potable water, and a boat launch. The shallow lake covers about 11 acres and is heavily stocked with rainbow trout; no motors allowed.

Drive past the campground along the west side of the lake to the Frog Lake Day-Use Area. Along with picnic tables and charcoal burners, enjoy stunning views of Mount Hood just across the water.

The day-use area at Frog Lake features a great view of Mount Hood.

Region 8 — Olallie Lake to Government Camp

Back on Highway 26 Heading North: After leaving the Frog Lake parking lot we'll top Wapanitia Pass and head downhill; look for some views of Mount Hood's massive form dead ahead. We'll pass by the first gas station we've seen in awhile along this stretch of the highway. It's about 5 miles from the pass to our next intersection with Oregon Highway 35.

INTERSECTION OF OREGON HIGHWAYS 26 & 35

⇨ **Note:** *If you haven't been here before, don't be afraid to pull over and consult the map. If it's winter time and Lolo Pass is closed, Highway 35 is the only way north to the City of Hood River. If you are strictly looking for scenery, Highway 35 is by far the most scenic route to the upper Hood River Valley and Region Nine to its end at the Bridge of the Gods.*

Even if you take Highway 35 to Hood River, I recommend you backtrack to Highway 26 and explore nearby Timberline Lodge, Trillium Lake, and Government Camp (the beginning of Region Nine) before heading to the north side of Mount Hood.

For those who choose to explore the Barlow Pass area and/or wish to bypass Lolo Pass, **turn right onto Highway 35 and after a couple of blocks, turn right at the sign showing the way to the "Pioneer Woman's Grave."** The road to the grave site is part of the old Barlow Trail and connects to Highway 35 at Barlow Pass. A shrine of sorts marks the spot where the woman's remains were discovered during road building in the 20th century. It's a good place to pause and reflect on the incredible hardships endured by travelers along the Oregon Trail.

Heading uphill past the grave, we'll come to a viewpoint (called Buzzard Point) with informational signs about glaciers on Mount Hood. A spring here runs into an ancient looking stone cistern. Just past the viewpoint, we'll arrive at **Barlow Pass and the PCT trailhead** and parking area. Past the road head for the old Barlow Trail, the road intersects Highway 35 where the Main Route turns left (west) on Oregon Highway 35, backtracking to rejoin Highway 26 West.

BARLOW PASS AREA: Elevation 4,157 ft.

The old Barlow Road heads downhill and due south from the pass. Those who wish to follow the path of the first wagon road across the Cascades can follow the rough road (border-line for passenger cars in dry conditions) for about 0.6 miles to the Devil's Half Acre Campground.

Northern Oregon Backroads Guide to the PCT

The road was named after **Samuel Barlow**, an immigrant from Kentucky. A quote attributed to Mr. Barlow reportedly went, "God never made a mountain but what He provided a place for man to go over or around it." Barlow's band of seven wagons set out from The Dalles in late September 1845 to find a feasible wagon route across the Cascades, avoiding the expensive and dangerous option of rafting down the Columbia River. Lolo Pass, on Mount Hood's western flank, was the only path across the mountains used by the early pioneers. While it was possible to drive livestock across Lolo, the way was too rough for wagons.

In early October 1845, Barlow and a small group of men scouted ahead of the wagons and believing they had glimpsed the Willamette Valley, returned to find another group of 23 wagons led by **Joel Palmer**. Palmer's group had trailed them hoping to follow Barlow's lead. The two groups combined forces to form a clearing party, opening the way to a ridge on the shoulder of Mount Hood known today as Barlow Pass.

Barlow and Palmer climbed high on the southern slopes of Mount Hood to scout for a way westward. Most of the wagons returned to

Hunting for tadpoles at Trillium Lake, Mount Hood in the background.

Region 8 — Olallie Lake to Government Camp

The Dalles while Barlow and Palmer continued on foot down the Sandy River to near the present-day town of Eagle Creek.

Petitioning the territorial legislature for $4,000 dollars for construction, Barlow was joined by Oregon businessman Phillip Foster in the construction and collection of tolls for the new road. Despite the huge ruts, mud, dust, and washouts, the road was instantly popular; in its first year of operation Barlow noted the passage of 152 wagons, 1,300 sheep, and 1,559 mules, horses, and cattle. The Barlow Road had a big impact on the future state of Oregon, completing the last leg of the overland **Oregon Trail**.

Sections of the Barlow Road east of Barlow Pass are still used by motor vehicles today and make for interesting exploration. The Barlow Trail Association sponsors a pioneer camp each year at White River Station along the Barlow Road. Usually held the second week in September, interpreters enact scenes from a typical pioneer camp of the 1840s. An old wagon is trailered in, providing a colorful backdrop for this historical site.

Back on Highway 26 Heading West: After leaving the Highway 35 intersection behind, look for a turn-off to the south (left) marking the road to Trillium Lake.

TRILLIUM LAKE AREA: Elevation 3,608 ft. at the lake's surface.

> ⇨ **Note:** *The turn-off to Still Creek Campground is about a mile northwest of the Trillium Lake turn-off on Highway 26. The two campgrounds are connected by a north-south forest road system that's popular with cross-country skiers when the snow flies.*

Beautiful Trillium Lake covers over 60 acres and provides good habitat for rainbow trout. A fishing pier is near the boat launch. Created by a dam across Mud Creek, the lake was built by the Oregon Department of Fish and Wildlife in 1960 but is now administered by the Forest Service. The **Trillium Lake Campground and Day-Use Area** are very popular and heavily used in the spring, summer, and fall. The campground has 57 sites, water, and vault toilets.

A detached camp with seven sites for tents lies on the southwestern end of the lake, across the dam. A loop trail around the lake's shoreline, some of it across boardwalks, is great for kids. Make sure and bring your camera to capture the huge views of Mount Hood across the lake's sparkling waters.

The grand entrance of the historic Timberline Lodge greets visitors year-round.

Back on Highway 26 Heading West: After leaving the Trillium Lake Road we'll head uphill and after about 1.5 miles we arrive at the turn-off to our right (north) to Timberline Lodge.

<u>TIMBERLINE LODGE:</u> Elevation 5,980 feet at the lodge.

> ⇨ **Note:** *The Pacific Crest Trail connects to the lodge via a short side trail.*

Construction of the grand old lodge of Mount Hood was begun in 1935 and opened to the public in February 1938. The building was a project by the Works Progress Administration. The WPA was a way to put depression era men to work, one of several ideas floated by the Roosevelt administration. Constructed of local stone and timbers, the Lodge attracts nearly 2 million visitors annually, drawn to the area for skiing, hiking, and sight-seeing opportunities.

Timberline has been operated by the Kohnstamm family since 1955. When **Richard Kohnstamm** took over operations, the Lodge was closed and in disrepair due to financial difficulties. The vibrant atmosphere at the Lodge today is a testament to Mr. Kohnstamm's dedication to restoring and maintaining the structure and promoting the sport of skiing. Timberline Lodge has the longest ski season in the nation thanks to the snowfields and glacier above the Lodge.

Region 8 — Olallie Lake to Government Camp

A heated swimming pool is open year-round, plus choose from two dining rooms and the Rams Head Bar. For reservations and information:

Timberline Lodge
503-272-3311 or timberlinelodge.com

Back on Highway 26 Heading West: The turn-off to Government Camp and the beginning of Region Nine is less than a block from the Timberline Lodge Road.

END OF REGION EIGHT

In Region Eight we've traveled from the foot of Mount Jefferson to the shadow of Mount Hood. Along the way we've explored the headwaters of the Clackamas River and now find ourselves in the Sandy River drainage. We'll stay on the west side of the Cascade Crest before crossing back over to the east side at Lolo Pass and descending the Upper Hood River Valley to the Columbia River and the Bridge of the Gods, where the PCT crosses into Washington State.

MAP R9.1: MAIN ROUTE

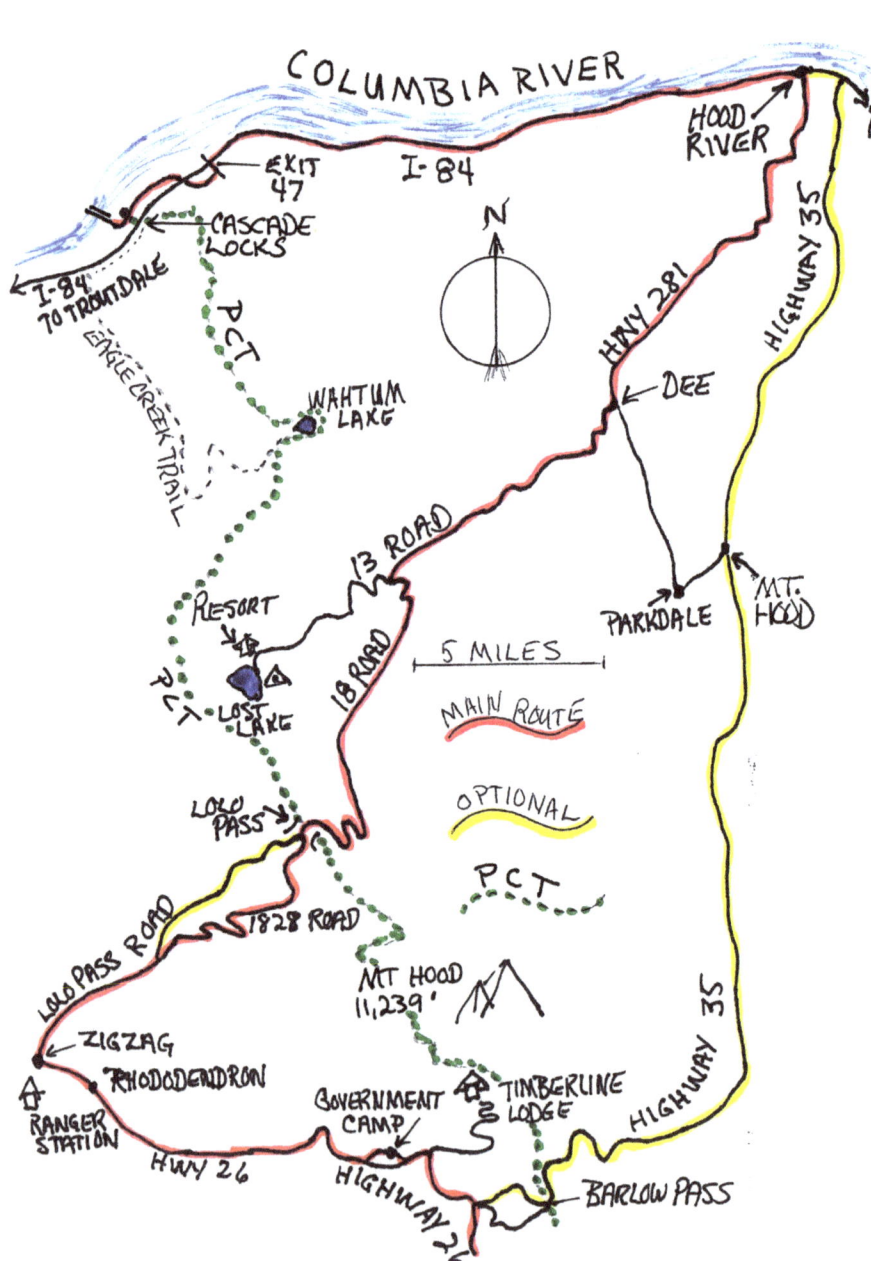

REGION NINE
Government Camp to the Bridge of the Gods

The beautiful Hood River Valley is orchard country. Many farmstands and specialty stores compete with wineries for tourists' attention.

"What a long, strange trip it's been."
— *The Grateful Dead*

Region 9 — Government Camp to Bridge of the Gods

ROUTE DESCRIPTION

Region Nine continues our exploration of Mount Hood's southern and western sides before following the Hood River north, to the Columbia River. This last stretch of the route is the most "civilized" of all the previous regions in this volume. Region Nine has more towns of various sizes than all the other regional descriptions combined. The bad news is this is the least "wild" of all the regional descriptions in the entire state of Oregon. The good news is there are plenty of good restaurants along the way.

Starting at the town of Government Camp, the Main Route heads west on Oregon Highway 26 to the town of Zigzag. From Zigzag we'll head northwest on the Historic Lolo Pass Road, following the Sandy River upstream 4 miles to our turn-off to Forest Road 1825 then Road 1828. We'll have a chance for a short hike along the western flank of Mount Hood, before arriving at Lolo Pass and an intersection with the Pacific Crest Trail.

From Lolo Pass, it's all downhill as we follow the 18 Road to its intersection with the Lost Lake Road. After an optional exploration of Lost Lake, the 18 Road continues down the West Fork of the Hood River to near where it joins the Middle and East Forks of the Hood River at Dee Flats. We'll follow the Dee Highway north to its meeting with Tucker Road, leading us into the City of Hood River.

After an exploration of the City of Hood River, we'll head downriver through the breathtaking Columbia Gorge to the town of Cascade Locks and the Bridge of the Gods. A short description of the nearby waterfalls and many hiking opportunities in the Cascade Locks area ends this volume.

RECOMMENDED MAPS FOR REGION NINE

The following maps are useful supplements to this guidebook.

- *Mount Hood National Forest Visitors Map*
- Benchmark Maps – *Oregon Road and Recreation Atlas*, pages 37 and 49

The Mount Hood National Forest Visitors Map is available at ranger stations and online at http://www.fs.usda.gov/mthood. Benchmark maps are available at bookstores, sporting goods stores, and on-line at benchmarkmaps.com.

⇦   *Sacajawea points the way west at Cascade Locks.*

Northern Oregon Backroads Guide to the PCT

OPTIONAL ROADS IN REGION NINE

There are no clearance or traction issues in Region Nine in good weather. Highway 35 is the obvious optional road to driving the Lolo Pass / 1828 Road north from Zigzag to the City of Hood River. Highway 35 offers stunning scenery, first crossing Barlow Pass, the stark and beautiful headwaters of the White River, and Bennett Pass before following the East Fork of the Hood River to the tiny town of Mount Hood. Before arriving at the Columbia River and the City of Hood River, Highway 35 takes the traveler through the Upper Hood River Valley with close-up views of Mount Hood to the south and distant Mount Adams in Washington State. Other places to explore on the mountain's northeast flanks would include the Cloudcap-Tilly Jane Historical District, Cooper Spur, and the southern terminus of the Mount Hood Railroad at Parkdale.

PCT ACCESS POINTS

Region Nine has three access points to the PCT.

1. The PCT passes above Government Camp and is accessible by a short trail from Timberline Lodge. It's 19 trail miles from Timberline Lodge to Lolo Pass.

2. The next point of road access to the PCT is at Lolo Pass. From Lolo Pass to Eagle Creek Trail, an alternate to the PCT at Wahtum Lake, it's 17 trail miles.

3. The end (or beginning) of the PCT in northern Oregon is at Cascade Locks on the Columbia River, where hikers cross the river via the Bridge of the Gods. From Wahtum Lake to the Bridge of the Gods, it's 16.5 trail miles via the Eagle Creek Trail alternative. By way of the PCT, it's 15.5 trail miles.

A BRIEF INTRODUCTION TO REGION NINE

The final regional description of *Volume Two* wouldn't be complete without paying homage to the dramatic landscapes created here by the interactions of fire and water. Over millions of years, vents located in Idaho, Washington, and eastern Oregon spewed liquid lava in waves, sometimes spaced by hundreds of thousands of years.

The multiple layers of the Columbia River Basalt flows ran hundreds of miles and repeatedly inundated this gap in the Cascade Range we call "The Gorge," building layer upon layer of basalt and rearranging the mighty Columbia River herself. Some headlands on the northern

Region 9 — Government Camp to Bridge of the Gods

Oregon coast are made up of **Columbia River Basalts**. The extent of the flows shows them to be **among the largest basalt formations of their kind in the world**.

Later on came the epic **Missoula Floods**, created by the repeated breaching of glacial dams that formed huge lakes in northwestern Montana. The massive walls of water unleashed when the ice dams fell, carved out huge chunks of eastern Washington State and sent it down the Columbia Gorge, depositing rocks from hundreds of miles away as the backwash ran up the Willamette Valley southward for miles.

Imagine the high walls forming today's Gorge brimming full of rolling rocks as big as buses, logs, and churning water and you can envision what it must have looked like. **Much of the deep topsoil of the Willamette Valley was transported from today's Washington State.** The scenery along the Gorge, where the never ceasing waters of the Columbia River have carved a way through the solid rock, is unparalleled in the American west with an ever changing panorama of light, clouds, and shadow.

Mount Hood is Oregon's tallest mountain at 11,249 feet. A majestic peak seen usually cloaked in snow when it's not wrapped in

Built by fire and carved by ice, Mount Hood is Oregon's tallest peak.

clouds, Mount Hood hosts hikers and skiers from the northwest and around the world. In clear weather, views of Mount Hood dominate the skyline for miles in every direction. This peak is also rated by vulcanologists as among the most likely Oregon mountains to erupt. The dramatic sweep of geography from Mount Hood's icy ramparts to the Columbia River contains some of the best orchard land in the country, taking advantage of the fertile soils and bountiful waters.

Beautiful scenery and rich resources have attracted people to this area for thousands of years; certainly the First People who populated this incredible joining of mountain and water had the same feelings and emotions we have as today's residents and visitors to this place. Squint your eyes a little and look down the Columbia Gorge on a misty morning and imagine a time gone by when ancient eyes looked upon the scene of our distant past in North America.

Morning light illuminates the mighty Columbia River near Cascade Locks.

Region 9 — Government Camp to Bridge of the Gods

ROADS IN ORDER OF TRAVEL

State Highway 26	We'll drive west from Government Camp to the town of Zigzag.
Lolo Pass / Forest Hwy. 18	From Zigzag we'll head north on this paved road about 4 miles to the intersection with Forest Road 1825.
Forest Road 1825	We're on this paved road for about 0.5 miles to the intersection with the 1828 Road.
Forest Road 1828	Rather than drive the 18 Road under the power lines, we'll head north on this paved road to Lolo Pass and rejoin Forest Hwy. 18 there.
Forest Hwy. 18 at Lolo Pass	The road turns to improved gravel for about 4 miles before becoming paved. We stay on the 18 Road to the intersection of Forest Hwy. 13.
Forest Hwy. 13	(This is the Lost Lake Road) We'll follow the West Fork Hood River north to the town of Dee and a meeting with Highway 281.
County Hwy. 281	We'll stay on Hwy. 281 to downtown City of Hood River where we'll turn west on Oak Street / Oregon Hwy. 30 to the on-ramp for Interstate 84 at Exit 62.
(The dreaded) I-84	The stretch run to Exit 47. Sorry, I know it's a freeway; the good news is it takes us along the awesome Columbia River.
Exit 47	We're still a couple of miles from Cascade Locks but we'll drive the rest of the way off of I-84.
Wyeth Road	The off-ramp arrives at Wyeth Road. We'll turn left, pass under the freeway, then turn right on old Highway 30 to Cascade Locks.
Hwy. 30 / Wa-Na-Pa Street	The main drag through Cascade Locks takes us to the Bridge of the Gods where the PCT crosses the Oregon state line.

Northern Oregon Backroads Guide to the PCT

ROAD NOTES – REGION NINE

Our exploration of Region Nine starts on the flanks of Mount Hood in the town of Government Camp and heads to the town of Zigzag.

Government Camp Area: Despite its rather official sounding name, Government Camp is a bustling little burg. Largely owing its modern existence to its proximity to Oregon's tallest mountain, "Govy" (pronounced GUH-vee), as the locals call it, caters to the ski crowd in the winter and tourists in the summer.

Located on a shoulder of the mountain above busy Highway 26, the wide main drag through town is lined with restaurants and other service businesses. There's a gas station and the Govy General Store along main street. The general store has a deli and extensive grocery items; ask them for the "I ♥ Govy" bumper sticker. Lodging in town ranges from high-end chalets to more humble condos and hotels.

Govy was originally established in 1849 by packers hired by the government of the time to supply forts with munitions and supplies. With the logistics of moving 400 wagons with 250 tons of cargo, the train made a late start from The Dalles on the Columbia River. With large parties of immigrants along the Barlow Road, forage for beasts was sparse for late season travelers. Forced to abandon

A small park greets visitors to Government Camp.

Region 9 — Government Camp to Bridge of the Gods

It's good food and friendly clutter at Charlie's.

some supplies because of the starvation of dozens of mules, 45 or more wagons were abandoned along the way with several being deposited at this site, later called Government Camp by the wagon pioneers traveling the Barlow Road. Over the years, there's been talk among the locals about changing the name to something less solemn and more befitting the Oregon town closest to the highest mountain in the state (and an active volcano), but the old name has stuck so far.

In winters of bountiful snow, skiers and snowboarders flock to Mount Hood. With most of the population of the Portland-Metro area less than a two-hour drive away, the streets and bars of Govy provide a lively scene when the snow is piled high. After ski season, the few year-round residents take a breath and enjoy the beautiful alpine surroundings.

Several good restaurants and bars in town serve the tourists and residents. Check out the **Ratskellar (The "RAT" as it's affectionately called)** for a great selection of beers and arguably the best pizza in town. An outdoor area allows well-mannered pooches. The bar and restaurant occupy the cavernous interior of the Bavarian-style building with a man-pit and a matching humongous wide-screen TV for sports fans.

MAP R9.2: CAMP CREEK TO LOLO PASS

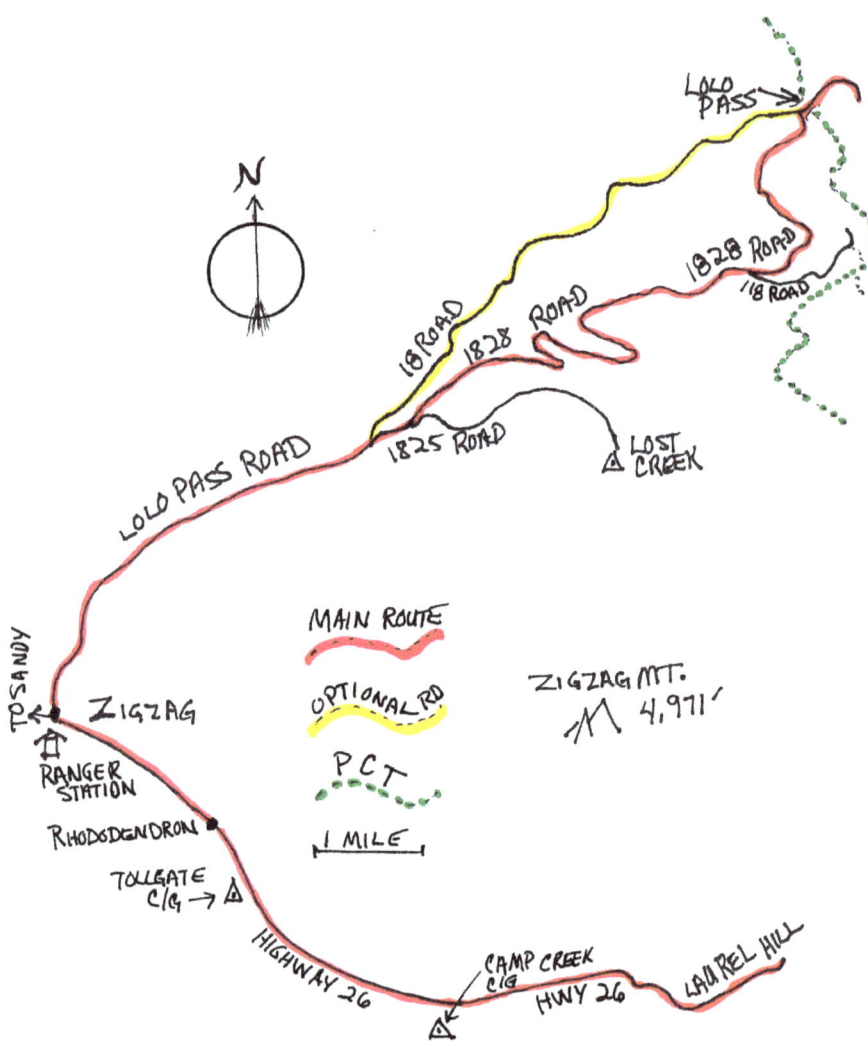

On the other side of the street is the legendary **Charlie's Mountain View**. Not much to look at from the outside, Charlie's serves up manly portions of hearty food for the after-ski crowd. The full bar is decorated with vintage ski memorabilia and several reminders of local history. This is the place to hang for the locals in the off season; the bar area is suitably cluttered with knicks and knacks, giving it a comfortable, well-used feel.

Region 9 — Government Camp to Bridge of the Gods

Heading West on Highway 26: After leaving Government Camp, the highway begins to head downhill. As we approach the top of **Laurel Hill**, we'll pass by the trailhead to popular Mirror Lake on our left; watch for cars turning and hikers alongside the highway. The hike to the lake is about 3 miles round-trip.

Laurel Hill was named by early travelers along the Barlow Road. The masses of nearly impenetrable thickets of rhododendrons were mistakenly called laurel after the closely related plant found in the eastern United States. Besides the rhody jungle, Laurel Hill presented the pioneers with the challenge of lowering their wagons and belongings down a 60-degree slope. Ropes were wrapped around trees and the wagons were slowly lowered in stages down the mountain.

Today's modern highway cuts through the solid rock of Laurel Hill and curves downhill, soon picking up the course of Camp Creek. As the highway begins to flatten out, we arrive at the turn to the left (south) to Camp Creek Campground.

Camp Creek Campground: This campground features 25 fee sites, water, and vault toilets. At the south end of the campground is a trail and a wooden foot bridge over Camp Creek leading to more trails. The campground is south of the highway and far enough away to shield some of the road buzz.

Back on Highway 26 Heading West: After leaving Camp Creek behind, we'll proceed another two miles west to a turn-off to our left (south) to Tollgate Campground.

Tollgate Campground: This Forest Service campground is situated in the big trees next to the **Zigzag River**. Unfortunately it's very close to the hum of Highway 26 so its not the quietest of places. The camp has an old feel to it and was a site on the Barlow Road where fees were collected. A shelter with a massive stone fireplace is next to a path heading down to the river. There are 15 fee sites with the usual amenities and **a trail connecting the camp with the nearby town of Rhododendron**.

The Town of Rhododendron: Named after the ubiquitous local flowers, the unincorporated town started out as a collection of summer cabins on the Zigzag River. Now a year-round community with the popularity of snow sports at nearby Mount Hood, the town supports a couple of very good restaurants and a well-stocked grocery store.

Northern Oregon Backroads Guide to the PCT

Skyway Bar and Grill has a pleasant outdoor garden and dining area.

If you showed up hungry, I highly recommend the **Rendevous (their spelling) Restaurant**. The food and service here are both superb; don't leave without trying one of their fantastic dessert offerings.

The other food place I recommend is located just out of the town proper, near milepost 43 on Highway 26 on the way to the town of Zigzag. The **Skyway Bar and Grill** has good food, a nice selection of northwest brews, and an outdoor dining area amid the collections of curios and garden art. Popular menu items include Mac and Cheese with "add-ons" and the pulled pork sliders.

Still heading west on Highway 26, about a mile past the Bar and Grill, we arrive at the town of Zigzag.

<u>THE TOWN OF ZIGZAG</u>: Elevation 1,425 ft.

There's not a whole lot to the town of Zigzag; the **Zigzag Ranger Station** is on the south side of Highway 26. Get maps and trail information at the ranger station; they also have large public bathrooms and potable water. There are plenty of hiking opportunities in the area, including the nearby trail up the Salmon River to a series of impressive waterfalls.

The venerable **Zigzag Inn** sits at the junction of Highway 26 and Forest Highway 18 / Lolo Pass Road. The restaurant and bar do a

Region 9 — Government Camp to Bridge of the Gods

thriving business in the winter and on summer weekends. The Inn is well known for their pizzas; try the Mediterranean style pie they call "Jimmy the Greek." The bar has a nice selection of wines and northwest beers.

At the entrance to the Lolo Pass Road is the **Zigzag Mountain House**, a good place for local hiking information, Zigzag T-shirts, and breakfast.

ZIGZAG TO THE CITY OF HOOD RIVER

From Zigzag, we'll take in the sights along the way to the City of Hood River.

Forest Highway 18 / Lolo Pass Road Heading North from Zigzag:

> ⇨ **Note:** *The Lolo Pass Road is paved from Zigzag to the summit where it rejoins the Guide's* Main Route. *The 18 Road follows the high tension power lines, and if you don't mind clear-cut scenery in front of you and snapping, crackling power lines above you, take this road rather than the 1828 Road. Personally I prefer the 1828 Road. Besides, my fellow travelers, this is the* Oregon Backroads Guide, *right?*

After leaving Zigzag, **we're on the paved 18 Highway a total of 4 miles to our first turn**. After crossing the Zigzag River, the highway

Please don't feed the bears!

Northern Oregon Backroads Guide to the PCT

The Bald Mountain Trail seems to lead into the sky. The flat valley to the left is Old Maid Flats, remnants of Mount Hood's last eruption.

from town crosses the Sandy River and follows the river northeast to the Mount Hood National Forest boundary. The 18 Road continues flanking the river to our first turn to the right onto the 1825 Road.

Intersection of Forest Roads 18 and 1825: The paved 1825 Road veers to the right from the Lolo Pass Road, closely following the Sandy River to an intersection with the 1828 Road at the bridge.

⇨ **Note:** *The Main Route does not cross the bridge.*

Intersection of Forest Roads 1825 and 1828: Elevation 2,020 feet.

Before heading off on the 1828 Road, you might opt into a short, side trip diversion.

Optional Side Trip to Lost Creek Campground: Cross the bridge and follow the 1825 road to the Lost Creek Campground turn-off. Here's your chance to look at the results of one of the **most recent eruptions on Mount Hood**. Erupting from a vent on Mount Hood's south side (Crater Rock), a wall of hot gas followed by debris flows of ice chunks, rocks, and trees seasoned with ash and pumice, was served up by the mountain in the 1790s. Today this area, known as

Region 9 — Government Camp to Bridge of the Gods

Old Maid Flats, supports scrubby trees amid the scattered, rounded rocks and pumiceous soil. When Lewis and Clark were making their way down the Columbia River, they noted a mass of quicksand-like debris clogging the mouth of the Sandy River, evidence that the debris generated by the eruption flowed more than 30 miles to the Columbia River. A nature trail near Lost Creek Campground has informational signs that explain this geologically interesting place.

On the 1828 Road Heading Northeast: The Main Route stays on the 1828 Road to Lolo Pass.

After leaving the bridge behind, the road edges along the Sandy River and crosses a bridge over a small stream. Stop here and follow the footpath upstream and find a small campsite and swimming hole; might be nice on a hot day. Back on the road, we stay on the pavement and begin to gain elevation as we zig and zag up the mountain. The road is in pretty good shape and follows the wilderness boundary to our right as we drive to an optional turn-off at the 118 Road and the **Top Spur trailhead**.

Optional 118 Road and the Hike to Bald Mountain: Elevation at intersection 3,535 ft. Top Spur trailhead elevation 3,925 ft.

It's an easy road to the trailhead and parking area. There's not much room to turn around at the trailhead so it's not suited for big motor homes or vehicles with trailers.

The trail to the overlook on the south side of Bald Mountain is about 1.8 miles round-trip and starts out from the parking lot, steeply climbing through a maze of tree roots; it can be a little muddy if the weather has been wet. After a short climb through the moss-draped forest, we'll arrive at the first intersection. Here we'll **cross the PCT and veer to the right and uphill along the Muddy Fork / Timberline Trail 600**. After a short walk on good tread through a shady forest, the trail emerges from the woods and opens into big views down to the Muddy Fork of the Sandy River. As the trail rounds a bend and comes to a viewpoint, elevation 4,395 feet, Mount Hood appears above us, seemingly close enough to touch. The 600 Trail continues around the mountain and eventually delivers the hiker back to Timberline Lodge.

Return to the parking lot, head back down the hill to the 1828 Road, turn right (uphill), and we'll arrive in short order at Lolo Pass.

Northern Oregon Backroads Guide to the PCT

MAP R9.3: LOLO PASS TO TUCKER PARK

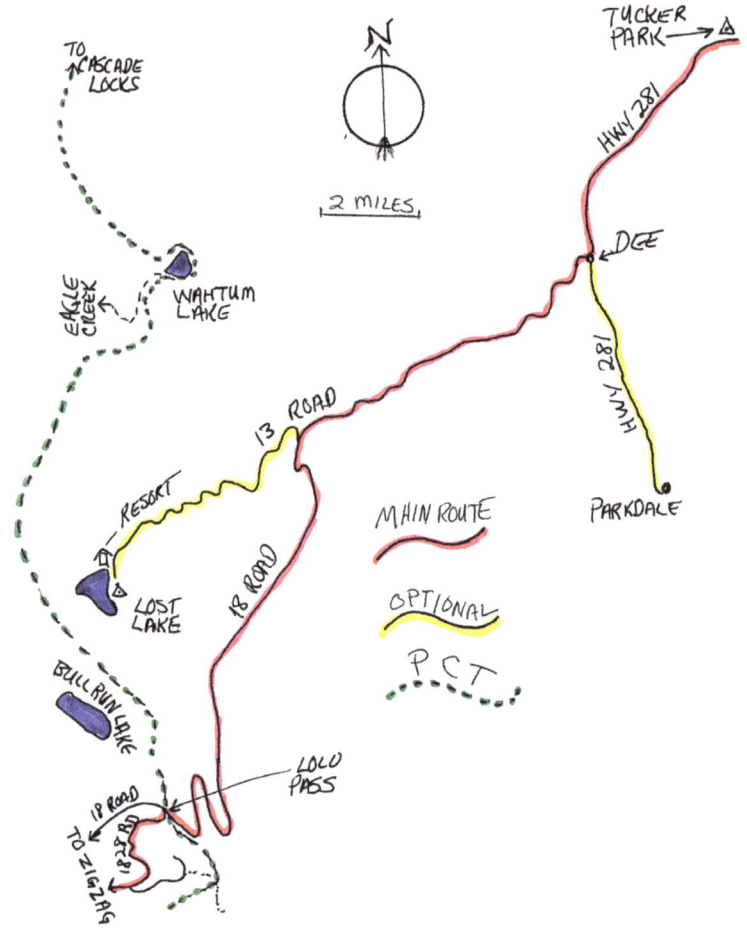

<u>**LOLO PASS AREA:**</u> Pass elevation 3,442 ft. PCT access.

This is the low-spot gap around Mount Hood used by men and critters for thousands of years before we dammed rivers and strung high tension power lines through here to fuel our insatiable hunger for electricity. **The PCT trailhead is well marked**, and there's enough room nearby for a compact camp. Before the Barlow Road was completed, this pass was used occasionally to drive livestock from the Columbia River to the Willamette Valley; the road was too rough to move wagons across. Today, the way is relatively smooth and easy but few travelers choose to drive this route, especially since Highway 35 around the eastern flanks of Mount Hood was opened, so don't expect a lot of traffic.

Region 9 — Government Camp to Bridge of the Gods

From the pass, the 18 Road becomes improved gravel and heads southeast and downhill. After crossing Elk Creek, the road swings north and zags south before crossing larger McGee Creek. McGee is a major contributor to the West Fork Hood River and heads directly north, as does the 18 Road.

The road breaks out of the forest canopy and becomes paved, with the power lines becoming visible to our left. While the acres of clear-cut adjacent to the power right-of-way are rather unattractive, the sunny openings host a variety of wildflowers, especially where there's water. The road jogs downhill, crossing the West Fork Hood River before coming to the intersection with Forest Highway 13 / Lost Lake Road.

INTERSECTION OF FOREST HWY. 18 & 13: Elevation 1,812 ft.

From this intersection the Main Route swings right and to the northeast along the 13 Road towards Dee.

Optional Road to Lost Lake: It's only three miles as the crow flies to Hood River County's Lost Lake but the curves in this twisty road double that mileage — no wonder this version of Lost Lake got the moniker. Lost Lake Resort and Campground are spread along the northeast shore of the 230-acre lake. The resort has a boat launch and day-use area. The marina rents rowboats and various other

Look for wildflowers in sunny forest openings.

Northern Oregon Backroads Guide to the PCT

Sasquatch stands guard at Lost Lake Resort's marina.

kinds of paddle craft; no motors allowed. There's a small store and along with rental cabins, the resort runs the campground. The massive campground is located away from the lakefront and features 148 fee sites with some spaces for tents only. The deep, clear lake is situated at an elevation of 3,158 feet and supports a healthy fishery for rainbow trout, kokanee, and the occasional brown trout. A three-mile trail circles the lake, and in clear weather the views of Mount Hood across the lake are stunning.

Back on Forest Highway 13 Heading Towards Dee: After leaving the Lost Lake intersection, the 13 Road continues downhill through the woods and hills before crossing the West Hood River and arriving at the orchard country of the upper Hood River Valley. The acres of orchards here at (upper) Dee Flats and the relatively flat areas above the Columbia produce a significant percentage of the nation's tree fruits, especially pears.

Follow the road through the farms (follow the signs) to where it dips down to cross the East Fork of the Hood River at the railroad siding marking Dee. After crossing the river, we travel over a set of railroad tracks and curve north to the "T" intersection with County Highway 281 where the [Main Route](.) turns left and heads north to the City of Hood River.

Region 9 — Government Camp to Bridge of the Gods

The Hood River Railroad's northern terminus is at Parkdale's Clear Creek Station. The horse and little girl are sculptures.

Optional Side Trip to Parkdale: The train tracks we just crossed belong to the **Hood River Railroad**. Originally a working, short-haul rail line, now a tourist attraction, the train runs on weekdays. The northern terminus of the rail line is in Hood River and the southern terminus is in **Parkdale**, five miles south of Dee. After crossing the tracks, instead of following the Main Route north (left), turn right and head south through more beautiful orchard country to check out the old **Clear Creek Rail Station** and the small town of Parkdale.

Heading North on County Highway 281: Elevation 960 ft. at Dee. As we leave Dee behind, the highway passes a group of houses; its near here the forks of the Hood River merge. We follow the Hood River downhill along this stretch, keeping left and heading downhill on County Highway 281. On our way to the City of Hood River, we'll pass Tucker County Park.

Tucker County Park is tucked next to the highway along the Hood River. With 93 sites, some with water and electricity, showers, and flush toilets, Tucker Park is heavily used by "boardheads" drawn to nearby Columbia Gorge winds. The park takes reservations; contact them at 541-386-4477.

Northern Oregon Backroads Guide to the PCT

Continuing north on 281 after leaving the park entrance, we quickly arrive at an **intersection with County Highway 282 where we keep left on Highway 281**. The highway crosses a bridge over the Hood River but just before we go over it, look for the entrance to the Apple Valley Country Store.

The **Apple Valley Country Store** is part of the Fruit Loop, a 35-mile driving tour of the region's fruit stands, wineries, and country stores. Featuring 32 individual businesses along the loop, Apple Valley Store is number 24 on the Fruit Loop.

Heading north on the 281 Road from Apple Valley store, we immediately cross the Hood River and wind our way downhill about a mile and a half to a four-way stop. **At the stop sign we'll follow Tucker Road to the right**, past the entrance to the **Western Antique Aeroplane and Automobile Museum**. The WAAAM is well worth a look, packed with many restored airplanes, cars, and trucks.

Tucker Road leads us to "The Heights" above Hood River proper. There are restaurants and big box stores along the road here. The road (follow 12th Street) continues downhill and takes us to **Oak Street, the main drag through downtown Hood River**. Turn right (east) to explore downtown Hood River. The Main Route turns left (west) on Oak Street and follows it to the on-ramp for I-84 at Exit 62.

THE CITY OF HOOD RIVER: Population estimate, 7,400 people. Elevation at the Columbia River about 100 ft.

This confluence of the Hood and Columbia Rivers has been a magnet to human beings for thousands of years. When Lewis and Clark came through here in 1805, there were thriving villages of Native Americans living along the rivers. They harvested the bounty of this rich land, moving to the high country in the heat of the summer to feast on huckleberries and harvesting the fish of the mighty Columbia in the fall.

Today's Hood River country still reverberates with its ancient and modern histories, both human and geological. The Gorge of the Columbia River is an awe-inspiring sight in the wispy dawn clouds of early morning. The opportunities for many different outdoor activities within an hour's drive from town draw those who seek to sail, windsurf, hike, cycle, kiteboard, fish, or just enjoy the scenery.

Besides the great scenery and nearby activities, Hood River offers itself up as the "Windsurfing Capital" of the United States. The

Region 9 — Government Camp to Bridge of the Gods

Find great beer and pizza at Double Mountain Brewery's taproom.

Gorge is the lowest point on the Pacific Crest Trail, and this gap funnels winds between lands on the eastern part of the Pacific Divide and the Pacific Ocean. In other words, this place blows (and I mean that in the best of ways) on a regular basis. Boardheads are a part of the Hood River crowd (and economy), and the culture fits nicely with the food and beer scene in town.

Full Sail Brewing has been a part of Hood River for many years and has a restaurant and bar near the waterfront. This brewery was among many northwest pioneers who, early on, promoted craft-style ales and northwest hops. Try a pint of their classic amber ale and a plate of reasonably priced appetizers (try the hummus plate) while you soak up the view.

Just uphill and two blocks east of Full Sail, look for the **Double Mountain Brewery and Taphouse** (8 Fourth Street), a family-friendly restaurant (until 9 p.m.). The taphouse offers yummy pizzas cooked in a 700-degree oven, great salads, and a wide selection of craft-brewed beers made on the premises. The brewery offers tours on weekdays and features live music on their indoor stage.

Forget trying to get a last-minute room around the valley during the **Hood River Valley Blossom Fest**. Held in mid-April, hoards of tourists descend on the Upper Hood River Valley to view the beauty of blossoming fruit trees growing at the foot of snow-covered Mount Hood.

Several lodging options in the area range from quaint B&Bs to the venerable **Hood River Hotel**. The very dog friendly Hood River Hotel is located in the heart of downtown within walking distance to some great eateries and shopping opportunities.

Heading West on I-84 from the City of Hood River: A note of apology to my readers; a large part of the reason I started mapping the backroads version of the Pacific Crest Trail was to avoid the interstates (I-5 in particular) and here we are back in the road race called Interstate 84. I rationalize it by the short distance and its proximity to the mighty Columbia. **If you would like to avoid the clutter and rush of traffic on I-84, drive across the toll bridge at Hood River and drive the Washington side** of the Gorge west to the toll bridge at Cascade Locks. The scenery is just as good and the laid-back towns on the Washington side have many charms.

I still recommend the Oregon side of the river (because it's in Oregon) even though it is a freeway. After all, it is the incredible Columbia freakin' River and you don't have to hold your breath as you cross the two extremely narrow toll bridges that hook up the Washington side with Oregon.

Kiteboarders get ready to fly at Hood River.

Region 9 — Government Camp to Bridge of the Gods

MAP R9. 4: CASCADE LOCKS - THE BRIDGE OF THE GODS

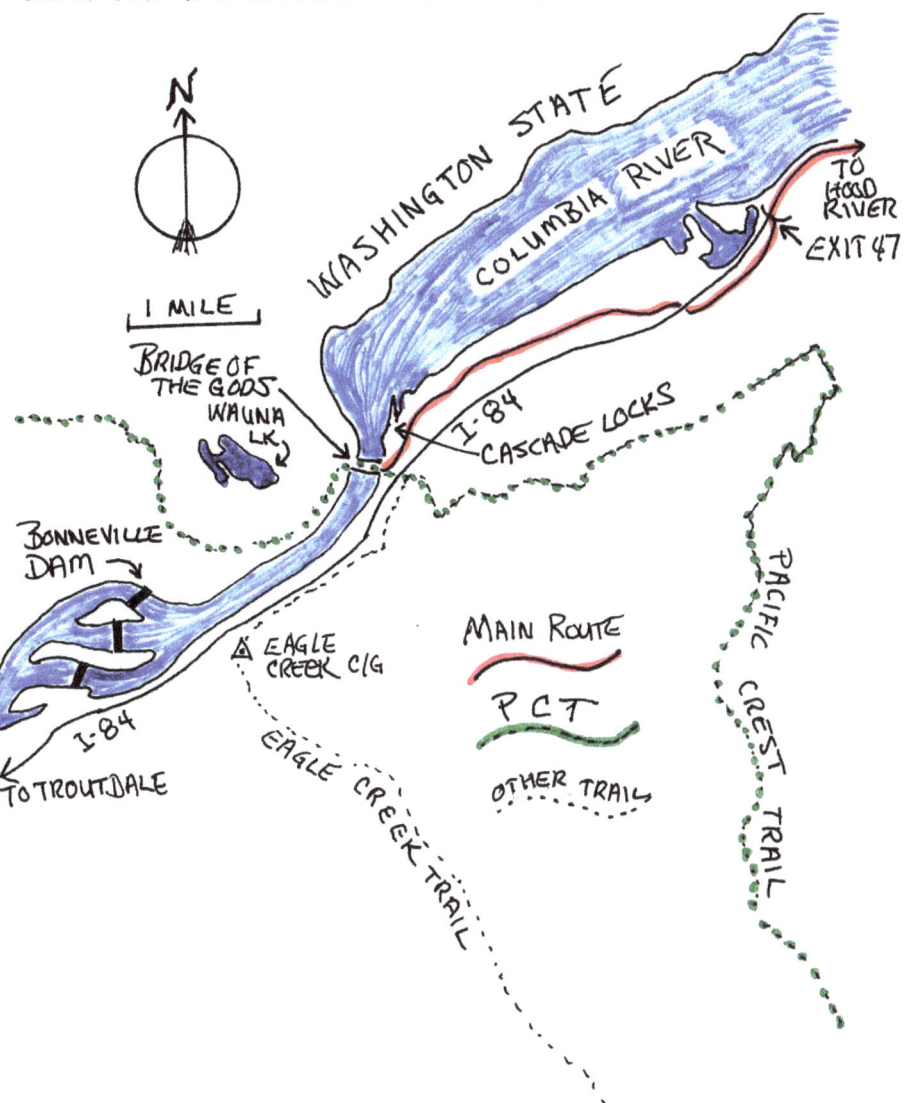

Along the way to Cascade Locks we'll pass **Viento State Park** on our right. The park has 55 sites with electricity and water and 15 tent sites. Viento means wind in Spanish and the state park is heavily used by wind sailors.

Still Heading West on the Dreaded I-84: Stay in the slow lane as you soak up the soaring ramparts rising above the "River of the West" along this stretch of the highway (and watch out for that semi).

★ *171* ★

Pieces of the original highway run through the Gorge. Constructed between 1913 and 1922, the **Historic Columbia River Highway**, designated Highway 30 through here, exists in segments adjacent to the freeway. Complete with arched bridges of intricate stonework and curving roads engineered to show off the natural beauty, sections are open to automobiles. Other pieces of the old highway have been converted to foot trails. Look for places along the freeway where the old road works are visible.

Exit 47: Here's our chance to get off the freeway and take a walk, too. The off-ramp takes us to a "T" intersection with Wyeth Road. The Main Route turns left and passes beneath the interstate and turns right (west) on the frontage road / Hwy. 30. As we approach Cascade Locks, Highway 30 crosses the freeway and enters the eastern part of town. At the stop sign we veer right on Wa-Na-Pa Street to the Bridge of the Gods and the western part of town.

Optional: Turn right at the "T" and pass under the tracks to a gated turn-around. Take a walk along the paved roadway to the western side of the peninsula and soak in the views. **A word of warning: Ticks are found along lowland waterways in Oregon.** Be sure to apply DEET to your boots, pant legs, ankles, and shins (especially in the spring and early summer) if you are hiking through tall grass and bushes along the Columbia.

CASCADE LOCKS AREA

The stories of the towns along this stretch of the river talk about the difficulties of moving people and freight across the **Columbia River Cascades**. The surrounding mountains are not particularly high (with the exception of Mount Hood) where they meet the river. Early (European) explorers and emigrants noted the large rocks and rapids marking this point along the Columbia, and the adjacent mountains became the "Mountains of the Cascades."

Pioneers rafted the perilous waters at risk of life and property. Later in the 19th century, steamboats plied the river above and below the rapids. The portage on foot was long, arduous, and dangerous, often along wood-planked catwalks suspended above the river. A narrow gauge rail line was laid along the portage portion making the movement somewhat easier.

Pursuing the dream of unfettered steamboat passage from the Pacific Ocean to the rapidly growing Inland Empire, Cascade Locks were built to raise and lower freighters, thus avoiding the rapids. Not long

Region 9 — Government Camp to Bridge of the Gods

after the locks were completed, the railroad extended a line through the gorge making the locks less useful. The construction of the **Bonneville Dam** in 1938 flooded the locks and made them obsolete.

Though the dates are not certain, it's evident that a massive landslide originating on the Washington side of the river created a natural dam across the Columbia River where the Cascades were (Bonneville Dam backs the river up, flooding the Cascades today). Look across the river at Table Mountain where you can still see the sheer cliffs marking the head of the monumental slide that gave birth to the First American's story of the **"Bridge of the Gods."**

As hard as it is to fathom, as we gaze across the broad Columbia, that a landslide of sufficient proportions could dam the river, the evidence is overwhelming that the Native story of a natural bridge across the river is indeed fact. When Lewis and Clark passed through in 1805, they noted tree stumps, some distance from shore that appeared to be drowned, and other visual evidence that water had backed up the river for some distance sometime in the past. Possibly triggered by an earthquake, the landslide and resulting blockage of the river must have been an awesome spectacle to behold by the people who were there.

The Bridge of the Gods crosses the Columbia River at Cascade Locks, marking the northern end of Oregon's Pacific Crest Trail.

Today's modern crossing of the Columbia, also called the Bridge of the Gods, is achieved by a metal bridge that looks like it was put together from a giant erector set. Not quite living up to its grandiose name, this ho-hum structure takes hikers on the Pacific Crest Trail across the Columbia River into Washington State and the end of this *Guide*.

The **Cascade Locks Marine Park** covers many beautifully manicured acres along the riverfront. There's a bronze statue of the Native woman Sacajawea who assisted Lewis and Clark in their exploration of the west, a day-use area, marina, a museum, boat launch, and ticketing for sight-seeing rides on the triple-decked **sternwheeler "Columbia Gorge."** Call 1-800-224-3901 for information and reservations.

MORE ACTIVITIES IN THE CASCADE LOCKS AREA

Don't forget to take the tour of the nearby waterfalls along the Oregon side of the Gorge, including amazing **Multnomah Falls**, Oregon's tallest waterfall. From Cascade Locks, drive west on I-84 to the well-signed **Exit 35, marking Old Highway 30** and the waterfalls. There are several falls in the vicinity, some right next to the road and others accessed by hikes of varying distance.

Eagle Creek Campground and trailhead are a couple miles west of Cascade Locks. **The Eagle Creek Trail is used by hikers on the PCT as an alternate** to the dry and nearly viewless section of the PCT from Wahtum Lake to the Gorge. The trail up the creek from the Gorge is heavily used and attracts day hikers to view the series of beautiful waterfalls and pools along the creek.

Nearby Bonneville Dam is also worth an exploration with September being the best time to view a variety of Salmon using the fish ladder to access upriver spawning areas.

Multnomah Falls is Oregon's tallest at 620 feet.

Northern Oregon Backroads Guide to the PCT

FOREST ROADS INDEX

13 Road / Lost Lake 155, 165–166

16 Road / Three Creek Lake 57, 64, 75, 78–79

18 Road / Lolo Pass 151–152, 155, 161–162, 165

42 Road 119–121, 131–132, 140

46 Road / Breitenbush River 97, 109-110, 129

46 Road / Cascade Lakes Highway 19-20, 22-24, 44, 46, 48-49, 57, 64-65, 68

57 Road 119-121, 134, 136, 139

58 Road 119, 121, 139–140

110 Road / Extension of the Skyline Road north of Olallie Lake 119, 121–122, 128–130

118 Road / Top Spur Trailhead 163

120 Road 131

141 Road 132

370 Road / Todd Lake Road to Three Creek Lake 57–58, 64, 71, 75

382 Road 75, 76

404 Road 102

500 Road / Santiam Wagon Road 58–59, 62, 64, 82, 84–85

514 Road / Irish and Taylor Lakes Road 19–20, 23, 35, 39–40

515 Road 104

600 Road

1028 Road 57, 59, 64, 82

1514 Road 79

1825 Road 151, 155, 162

1828 Road 151–152, 155, 161–163

2067 Road 59

2660 Road 121, 140

2067 Road 59

2257 Road 91–92, 97, 100, 102–104

2261 Road 102, 104

2267 Road 91, 97, 100

2690 Road 57, 64, 85–86

4220 / Oregon Skyline Road 91–92, 97, 110, 112–113, 119–122, 125–127, 129

4230 Road 129

4240 Road 121, 131–132

4245 Road 132

4250 Road 132

4280 Road 134

4290 Road (Region 5) 19–20, 22, 24, 37

4290 Road (Region 8) 121, 140

4601 Road 75

4625 Road / Elk Lake Loop 68

4635 Road 23, 44

4636 Road 19, 22–23, 40–42, 44

4690 Road 91–92, 119, 129

5815 Road / Odell Butte 24

5820 Road 136, 139

5890 Road 119, 121, 139–140

5897 Road 23

5898 Road 23

Index

PLACES, PLANTS & NAME INDEX

45th Parallel 132

A

Amanita rubescens, mushroom 101–102
Ashland 2
Apple Valley Country Store 168

B

B&B Fire 84
Bald Eagles 27
Bald Mountain Trail 162–163
Barlow Toll Road 119, 143, 145, 156–157, 159
Barlow Pass (PCT trailhead access) 119–120, 143–144, 151
Barlow, Samuel 144
Barlow Trail Association 145
Beach Day-Use Area 53, 66–67
Belknap Crater 96
Bend (the city of) 20, 48–49, 57–58, 66–67
Bennet Pass 152
Betty Lake 32–33
Big Cove Campground 44
Big Lake 57, 62, 85
Big Lake Campground 85–86
Big Lake West Campground 85
Big Meadows Horsecamp 91, 100
Big Meadows Road (2267 Road) 91, 97, 100
Black Butte Ranch 80
Blue Box Pass 140
Bobby Lake 34

Bob Marley 117
Breitenbush Campground 112
Breitenbush Lake (PCT trailhead) 91–92, 97, 112, 129
Breitenbush Lake Road / 4220 Road 91–92, 97, 110, 112–113, 119–122, 125–127, 129
Breitenbush Hotsprings 110, 112
Breitenbush River 91, 97, 107–110
Bridge of the Gods 143, 151–152, 155
Broken Top Mountain 50, 57, 71–74, 76, 78
Broken Top Road / Trailhead 74
Brook Lake 128
Buzzard Point 143

C

California 2, 5, 7
Camp Creek 159
Camp Creek Campground 159
Camp Pioneer (Boy Scout) 103
Camp Ten 123
Canyon Theater 107
Cascade Lakes Highway (Forest Hwy 46) 19–20, 22–24, 44, 46, 48–49, 57, 64–65, 68
Cascade Locks 151–152, 155, 170
Cascade Mountains 2, 5–6
Cave Junction 3
Cedars Restaurant and Bar 108
Century Drive 48

★ 177 ★

Northern Oregon Backroads Guide to the PCT

Charlton Butte Fire 38, 40
Charlton Lake (PCT trailhead) 19–21, 23, 37
Charlie's Mountain View 157–158
Chinquapin Point 28
Circle Tree 32–34
City of Hood River 143, 151–152, 155, 161, 166–170
Clackamas Lake (PCT access nearby) 119, 129, 132–133
Clackamas Lake Campground 132–133
Clackamas Lake Ranger Station (historic) 132–134
Clackamas River 132
Clear Creek Station 167
Clear Lake (Linn County) 92, 94–95
Clear Lake Resort (Linn County), 95–96
Clear Lake (Wasco County) 119, 140
Clear Lake Campground (Wasco County) 140
Cloudcap-Tilly Jane 152
Cold Spring Campground (riparian area) 57, 82
Cold Water Cove Campground 96
Colorado Avenue 59
Columbia River 8, 144, 151–152, 154–155, 163, 166, 168, 170
Columbia River Basalts 152
Columbia River Highway (historic) / Highway 30 155, 172

Columbia Gorge 151–154, 168, 170
Cooper Spur 152
Cove Day-Use Area 138
Cow Meadow Campground 48
Crane Prairie Reservoir 20, 24, 46, 48
Crane Prairie Campground 48
Crane Prairie Resort 48
Crater Ditch Trailhead 73
Crater Lake 7
Crater Rock 162
Crescent Cut-Off Road 19, 24
Crescent Lake Junction 24
Crook Glacier 74
Cultus Lake 44
Cultus Lake Campground 44–45
Cultus Lake Resort 44–45
Cultus Lake Road 23–24, 46, 49
Cultus Mountain 44

D

Davis Lake 19, 24, 48
Deer Lake 44
DEET 34
Dee (town, flats) 151, 155, 165–166
Dee Highway / Highway 281 155, 166–168
Dee Wright 62–63
Dee Wright Observatory 7, 57, 59, 61–62, 82
Deschutes National Forest 22, 38, 40–41, 80
Deschutes River 28, 48, 52, 59, 78

Index

Detroit Lake 100, 106–107, 109
Detroit Lake (town of) 91, 97, 107–109
Detroit Lake Ranger Station 91, 109
Devil's Half Acre Campground 144
Devils Lake 7, 57, 68
Devil's Lake Campground 68
Diamond Peak 25, 27
Double Mountain Brewery 169
Driftwood Campground 77
Druids 34

E

Eagle Creek Trail (alternate to the PCT) 152
Eagle Creek (town of) 145
Eagle Peak 26
East Fork Hood River 151–152, 166
East Hanks Lake 42–43
Elk Creek 165
Edna Lake 41
Elk Lake 17, 22–23, 46, 53, 55, 57, 62, 64, 66
Elk Lake Campground 67–68
Elk Lake Loop Road 52
Elk Lake Resort (PCT access nearby) 49, 64
Emigrant Pass 25
Erma Bell Lakes 41

F

Fay Lake 91–92, 97, 102
Fir Lake 103
Fish Lake (Olallie Lake area) 127
Fish Lake Day-Use Area 93–94
Fish Lake Remount Station (historic) 92–93
Foster, Phillip 145
Frog Lake Campground 142
Frog Lake Day-Use Area 142
Frog Lake Trailhead for the PCT 119–120, 140, 142
Fruit Loop 168
Full Sail Brewing 169

G

Gerdine Butte 37
Glaciers, Ice Age 6
Gold Lake 25
Gold Lake Campground 24, 30
Gold Lake Road 24, 30
Gone Creek Campground 138
Government Camp (the town of) 119, 121, 136, 143, 146, 151–152, 155–158
Govy General Store 156
Graham, Joe 133
Grateful Dead 149
Great Spring 95
Green Lakes Trail 73

H

Hanks Lakes 39
Happy Valley 75
Head Lake (PCT trailhead) 125–126
High Cascades 5
Highway 20 59, 64, 82, 91–92, 97, 99–100
Highway 22 91–92, 97, 100, 104, 106, 109

Highway 26 119, 121, 140, 142–143, 145, 151, 155, 159–160
Highway 30 155, 172
Highway 35 121, 143, 152
Highway 58 19, 22–24, 26, 30, 32, 48
Highway 97 48, 58–59
Highway 126 92–93, 96
Highway 242 (McKenzie Pass Highway) 57, 61, 64
Highway 281 (Hood River County) 155, 166–168
Hogg Rock 99, 106
Hogg, Thomas Egenton 99, 106–107
Hood River (the stream) 151, 167–168
Hood River (city of) 143, 151–152, 155, 161, 166–170
Hood River Hotel 170
Hood River Railroad 167
Hood River Valley 167
Hood River Valley Blossom Fest 169
Hoodoo Ski Bowl 57, 85–86
Hoodview Campground 138
Hoover Campground 105
Horsefly Lake 34
Horseshoe Lake 113
Horseshoe Lake Campground 113
Hosmer Lake 52
Howkum Lake 34
Humbug Campground 110

I

Irish Lake (PCT trailhead) 19, 22–23, 38–42
Ice Age 6
Ice Cap Campground 97
Idanha (the town of) 106
Illinois Valley 3
Interstate 84 (the dreaded I-84) 155, 170
Islet Point Campground 36

J

Jefferson Park (Whitewater Creek Trail) 105
Joe Graham Horse Camp (PCT trailhead) 120–121, 134
Jude Lake 127

K

Kansas 2
KC's Cafe 108
Klamath Mountains 3
Kohnstamm, Richard 146
kokanee 29, 66, 85, 106, 166
Koosah Falls 92, 96–97, 100

L

Lake Timpanogas 25
Laurel Hill 159
Lava Camp Lake (PCT access nearby) 61
Lava Lakes 49
Lava Lake Campground 50
Lava Lake Resort 50
Lewis and Clark 168
Little Crater Lake (PCT access nearby) 119–120, 138–140,

Index

Little Crater Lake Campground 140
Little Cultus Lake Campground 19, 42-44
Little Fawn Group Camp 68
Little Lava Lake 52
Little Lava Lake Campground 52
Little Three Creek Lake 77, 78
Lolo Pass (PCT trailhead) 143, 144, 152, 155, 163, 164
Lolo Pass Road / Road 18 151–152, 155, 161–162, 165
Los Agaves Cafe 80, 81
Lost Creek Campground 162–163
Lost Lake (Hood River County) 151, 165
Lost Lake Resort and Campground (Hood River County) 165–166
Lost Lake Road (Hood River County) 151, 165
Lost Lake (Linn County) 91, 100
Lost Lake Campground (Linn County) 91, 100
Lower Lake 127
Lower Lake Campground / Trailhead 126–127
Lower Marilyn Lake 30

M

Mallard Marsh Campground 53
Many Lakes trailhead 19. 39, 43
Marilyn Lakes trailhead 24, 30
Marion Forks Campground 92, 97, 103–104
McGee Creek 165

McKenzie Bridge (town of) 61, 94, 96
McKenzie Pass / Hwy. and PCT trailhead 7, 57, 59-62, 66, 82
McKenzie Pass Wagon Road 60
McKenzie River 89, 94-97
McKenzie River Trail 94
Medford 6
Meditation Point Campground 139
Middle Fork Hood River 151
Middle Fork Ranger District 22
Middle Fork Willamette River 25, 36
Middle Hanks Lake 43
Minto Pass 101
Mirror Lake 159
Misery Creek 106
Missoula Floods 6, 153
Monon Lake 113–114
Montana 6, 153
Mount Adams 152
Mount Bachelor 19, 46, 49–50, 65, 67
Mount Hood 5, 7, 136, 143–144, 146, 151–154, 163, 166
Mount Hood (town of) 152
Mount Hood National Forest 120, 151, 162
Mount Hood Railroad 152
Mount Jefferson 5, 80, 102–105, 113, 120
Mount Jefferson Wilderness 91, 104, 109
Mount McLoughlin 5–6
Mount Saint Helens 6

★ *181* ★

Northern Oregon Backroads Guide to the PCT

Mount Shasta 3
Mount Washington 60, 84
Mud Creek 145
Muddy Fork Sandy River 163
Multnomah Falls 174–175
Mysterious Circle Tree of Betty Lake 32–34

N

Nash, Wallis 107
Nighthawks 125
North Arm Campground (PCT access nearby) 139
North Fork Breitenbush River 112–113
North Fork of the Middle Fork Willamette River 36
North Fork Tumalo Creek 57
North Matthieu Lake 61
North Santiam River 91, 101, 106–107
North Sister Volcano 57–58
North Tumalo Creek 57, 75
North Waldo Campground 19, 23, 35, 39

O

Oak Fork Campground (PCT access nearby) 136, 138
Oak Fork Clackamas River 132–134, 136, 138
Oakridge 25–26, 36
Oak Street 155, 168
Odell Butte 24
Odell Butte Lookout 24
Odell Creek Campground 28
Odell Lake 19, 26, 27

Odell Lake Lodge 28
Olallie Butte 125
Olallie Lake 89, 91–92, 106, 114, 119, 122, 125
Olallie Lake Day-Use Area 122
Olallie Lake Guard Station 122, 126
Olallie Lake Resort (PCT trailhead) 91, 97, 119, 124–126
Olallie Lakes Scenic Area 114, 119, 122
Olallie Meadow 128
Olallie Meadow Campground 128–129
Old Maid Flats 162–163
OR-7 5
Oregon Pacific Railroad 106–107
Oregon Skyline Road / 4220 Road 91–92, 97, 110, 112–113, 119–122, 125–127, 129
Oregon Trail 145
Osprey Point 46

P

Pacific Crest Trail 7–8, 19, 22, 26, 37, 40–41, 57, 59, 61–62, 66, 85–86, 97, 101, 105, 112–113, 119–122, 124–125, 134–136, 139–140, 143, 146, 151–152, 155, 163–164, 169
Pacific Ocean 169
Palmer, Joel 144–145
Parkdale 152, 167
Paul Dennis Campground 123–124
Pebble Bay Campground 28

Index

Pengra Pass 26
Peninsula Campground 122–123
Pika Lake 103
Pine Point Campground 139
Pine Ridge 103
Pioneer Woman's Grave 143
Pleistocene Era 5
Presley Lake 104
Princess Creek Campground 27–28
Point Campground 68
Portland General Electric 137
Pussypaws 84–85

Q
Quinn River 46
Quinn River Campground 46

R
Rams Head Bar 147
Ratskellar 157
Rendevous Restaurant 160
Rhododendron (town of) 159
Riverside Campground 104
Rock Creek Campground 46
Rockies 2
Roundabouts 59
Russ Lake 127

S
Sahalie Falls 89, 91–92, 96–97, 100
Salt Creek 25, 30
Salt Creek Falls 18–19, 26
Salt Creek Pass 25
Sandy River 7, 145, 151, 162–163

Santiam Junction 91–92, 97, 99–100
Santiam Pass (trailhead for the PCT) 57–58, 62, 79, 89, 91, 97, 99, 106
Santiam Wagon Road 58–59, 82, 84–85, 94
Sasquatch 166
Scott Pass 61
Seattle 2
Shadow Bay Campground 34
Shelter Cove Resort 20, 26, 29–30
Siskiyou Mountains 2–3
Sisters (town of) 7, 57–59, 73, 76, 78–82
Sisters Folk Festival 81
Sisters Hops Festival 81
Sisters Outdoor Quilt Show 81
Sisters Rodeo 81
Skyline Road / 4220 Road 91–92, 97, 110, 112–113, 119–122, 125–127, 129
Skyline Trail 7
Skyway Bar and Grill 160
Soda Creek Campground 57, 69
South Campground 53
South Sister Volcano 6, 7, 46, 50, 67, 71
Sparks Lake 57, 69
Sparks Lake Day-Use Area 57, 69
Spoon Lake 113
Still Creek Campground 145
Summit Lake 120, 128, 132
Sunset Cove Campground 28

Sunset View Day-Use Area 68
Suttle Lake 59

T

Tam McArthur Rim 57, 76–77
Tam McArthur Trail 77–78
Taylor Burn 23, 38, 40
Taylor Burn Guard Station 41
Taylor Lake (PCT trailhead) 19, 22–23, 38–41
The Dalles 144–145, 156
Three Creek Campground 77
Three Creek Lake 57–58, 71, 75, 77–78
Three Creek Meadow Campground 76, 78
Three Fingered Jack 80
Three Sisters volcanoes 6, 71, 76, 79, 92
Three Sisters Wilderness 43, 66, 71, 84
Timberline Lodge (PCT trailhead) 119–121, 136, 143, 146–147, 152, 163
Timothy Lake (PCT trailhead) 119, 121, 129, 134, 136
Timothy Lake Trail 136
Tiny Lake 34
Todd Creek Horsecamp 71
Todd Lake 57–58, 73
Todd Lake Trailhead / Day-Use Area 57, 64, 71–73
Tollgate Campground 159
Top Spur Trailhead / Bald Mountain Trail 162–163
Torrey Lake Trailhead 40
Trapper Creek 27

Trapper Creek Campground 26–27
Triangle Lake Campground 127
Trillium Lake 120, 143–145
Trillium Lake Campground and Day-Use Area 145
Tucker Park (Hood River County) 167
Tucker Road 151, 168
Tuya Volcanoes 99
Twin Lakes trail 142
Twins, the 37

U

Upper Arm Day-Use Area 109
Upper Hood River Valley 143, 152, 166, 169
Upper Marilyn Lake 30

V

Velveeta Point 50
Viento State Park 171

W

WAAAM (museum) 168
Wahanna Lake 40
Wahtum Lake 152, 174
Waldo Lake 19–20, 26, 34–36, 38
Waldo Lake Road 19, 22–24, 32
Waldo Lake Trail 34, 36
Waldo Lake Wilderness 36
Wa-Na-Pa Street 155, 172
Wapanitia Pass (PCT trailhead) 119, 121, 136, 142–143
Warm Springs Reservation 112, 122

Index

Warm Springs River 131
Washington State 2, 6–8, 153, 170
West Cultus Lake Campground 44
Western Cascades 5
West Fork Hood River 155, 165–166
West Hanks Lake 43
West Pinhead Butte 130
Whispering Falls Campground 106
White River 119
White River Station 145
Whitewater Creek Road 104–105
Whychus Creek 78–79
Wikiup Reservoir 24, 48
Willamette National Forest 92
Willamette Pass 2, 5, 19, 24–26
Willamette Pass Ski Area 26
Willamette Valley 6, 25, 144, 153
Windy Point 60
Winopee Trailhead 45
Works Project Administration 146
Wright, Dee 62–63
Wyeth Road (Exit 47) 155, 172

Y

yurts 123

Z

Zigzag 151–152, 155, 160–161
Zigzag Inn 160–161
Zigzag Mountain House 161
Zigzag Ranger Station 160
Zigzag River 7, 159, 161

Passenger window wildlife with Tam McArthur Rim in the distance.

"That was fun! Let's go again!"

AFTERWORD

I would like to thank all of my readers and those who have joined me on this "Twisting Journey" through Oregon's high country. Oregon is blessed with a geological and biological diversity seldom matched on planet Earth. The descriptions in this book are just the highlights of the interesting and diverse landscapes of northern Oregon's Cascade Range leaving plenty of places to explore for the adventurous.

Writing about and investigating this beautiful landscape has been an adventure spanning many years, and along the way, I've developed a deeper love for my adopted state and an appreciation for the land and all of the interesting creatures (plants and animals) that inhabit it.

My companion volume to this book takes the traveler on an exploration of southern Oregon's high country and road connections to the Pacific Crest Trail, including the ancient Siskiyou Mountains of northern California and southern Oregon. Like this volume, it ties in the human history of the region along with the geological and natural world aspects of the southern Oregon region. Look for **A Twisting Journey: Southern Oregon Backroads Guide to the PCT** in bookstores or online at OregonBackroads.com. Keep on ramblin'!

— Ed McBee

www.ingramcontent.com/pod-product-compliance
Lightning Source LLC
Chambersburg PA
CBHW051546010526
44118CB00022B/2595